I0801874

Acting on Clutter

Kammie Richter
Marilyn Myers
Bev Johns

TRUTH BOOK PUBLISHERS

ISBN: 978-1-946598-03-5

Truth Book Publishers
www.truthbookpublishers.com
truthbookpublishers@yahoo.com

Printed in the United States of America.

Dedicated to our sisters in Lambda State of Delta Kappa Gamma who brought us together and encouraged us to write this book.

Table of Contents

Introduction

Erika's husband and her two teenage children were tired of the cluttered kitchen and bathroom counters and the basement that was hard to walk in. While the house was dusted and vacuumed, Erika just could not bear to part with much of it.

Erika worked full time and was smart enough to realize that her classroom where she was a teacher was also cluttered. Alicia, her friend, asked Erika if her husband and children would help her. Erika replied that the problem was hers. They were more than willing to help her but she always made excuses about why she did not have time to get rid of all the clutter. She had more important things to do than clean. Alicia was not sure how she could help Erika. Erika told Alicia her family was considering a family meeting to discuss an intervention for her because she had just too many items with no place to put it.

Have you ever thought your family might want to call an intervention for you because you just have too much stuff? You want to start cleaning but you do not know where to start. Congratulations, you have taken the first step. You are reading this book to help you get started. You have recognized that you need help.

This book is designed to provide you with practical step by step directions on how to get your life back in control and to be clutter free.

In a *Redbook* survey conducted with 1,000 women 80% consider themselves organized but 72% still spend five minutes and some up to 20 minutes looking for misplaced items every day. The top three types of clutter included a junk drawer, an overstuffed closet, and piles of paper. Thirty percent of those in the survey reported having a whole room that is just for stuff that has no other spot. Because of chaos and clutter, 45% of individuals get charged for being late for paying a bill. (Rollins, 2016).

This useful guide outlines the reasons why we should declutter often and provides the practical tips you need to do it. Decluttering is a lifelong endeavor and we will explain how to approach it this way.

We all realize what we need to do to free ourselves from all the stuff we accumulate, but realization does not translate into action. This book not only provides you with the knowledge but also provides you with the action steps you can take to become clutter free.

Checklists are provided for each chapter and suggested actions are provided. This book is written by three women educators who have had to downsize several times in their lives and have learned the importance of accepting the process as a way of life. The book includes case examples throughout.

References:

Rollins, M. (Editor), 2016. Spill your secrets. *Redbook, September*, 2016. P. 15.

Chapter One
Downsizing as a Way of Life

Linda, a school teacher, loved to lead the simple life. She found great joy in the little things in life. She was a goal-setter who cleaned as she went. She had small closets so when she purchased something new she discarded another item.

Linda's classroom was neat and well organized. She taught her students that before you go home each day, you clean out your desk and discard what you do not need. In the summer she loved to travel and she took wonderful trips to Europe, among other places. She traveled light with only carry-on luggage and took a small additional empty bag that she could fold up to use for any souvenirs she purchased for others.

One summer a fellow teacher, Analise, invited her to go to Hong Kong for two weeks with her. Linda readily agreed and knew Analise was very congenial. The two talked about packing and Linda explained she was going to travel light.

The morning they were to catch their flight they met at the airport. Imagine Linda's surprise when Analise showed up with a carry-on bag plus two large bags to check, in addition to a large empty fold-up bag to bring home all of her purchases. Analise had packed two changes of clothes for each day, five pairs of shoes, and numerous cosmetic items.

Linda had accepted the simple life and was very organized and only got what she needed. Analise, on the other hand, was consumed by material items and had to have many choices of clothing and jewelry. She cluttered the room with the stuff she brought on the trip and then kept buying more items. Linda quickly figured out that she would not be traveling again with Analise.

We probably all know people who lead the simple life and do not have a lot of objects. Moving is easy for them, traveling is easier for them, and as we look at them we think that they live the easy good life. We know those individuals who are very well organized and everything they have is in its place. We wonder how they do it and we are envious that their life and surroundings are simple. They make it look easy.

It is not always easy, especially if we love things and love to accumulate things. We do not want to throw anything away because we may need it in the future. It can only become easy for us to purge if we adopt the philosophy that we will set a goal to make downsizing a way of life. We can take basic steps to make downsizing a habit one day at a time. We must adopt the adage; an ounce of prevention is worth a pound of cure. We have to talk ourselves through those frequent crises we face where we tell ourselves we just have to have that one item. We have to set small goals each day. Lastly, we have to elicit the help of others in meeting our goals and we have to learn from those individuals.

One Day at a Time

After watching the summer Olympics in 2016 we are in awe about how Michael Phelps can swim so extraordinarily, or how Simone Biles can jump so exquisitely. They practiced daily even on the days they did not feel like practicing because they knew that the more they did it, the better they would get at it.

If you want to simplify your life from clutter, it takes practice every day. We have to try to do at least a little bit. We cannot make excuses. When you do even a small amount each day it is more likely that cleaning will become a way of life for you. Doing a little bit each day provides practice and makes it easier each time you do it.

We may find ourselves guilty of procrastination. We look for excuses for why we cannot clean that drawer out or do not want to even go up into our attic. The world is full of procrastinators, and although they may be very talented individuals they may never accomplish their goals because they consistently find other things to do. It is all a matter of priorities. Those who accomplish a great deal are persistent. They take one day at a time and keep their eye on the goal and work toward it by persevering and not making excuses.

Catch Yourself When You Are Making Excuses

Successful individuals do not make excuses; they keep going. We live in a society today where everyone has excuses and others must be to blame. Unfortunate things happen to us and often it is out of our control, but we can control our response to those bad things. When someone asks us, is the glass half empty or half full? It is all about how we perceive things and what our attitude is. If we are positive that we can turn things around and live a clutter free life, then we can do it. If we believe that we will always live in a messy house and just have too many things and cannot throw anything away, then that is exactly what will happen to us.

Have you ever caught yourself making these excuses about why you have too much stuff?

- My husband is so messy; I just cannot clean up after him.

- I am involved in too many projects; there is no way I can keep everything organized.

- I have a small house; I just do not have any place to put things.

- I have three kids; there is no way I can possibly have a neat house.

- I just do not have the time to clean out anything.

When you catch yourself making an excuse, stop and reflect on what you are doing. You are standing in your own way of success in decluttering. If you want to take control of your life, identify the excuses, and do not allow them to make your decision. Take control.

An Ounce of Prevention is Worth a Pound of Cure

We work to prevent heart disease by taking better care of ourselves. We work to keep our car in good working order by taking it in for routine maintenance. These are preventive strategies. If we perform certain actions as we go, we can prevent something going wrong or at least reduce the likelihood of something going wrong.

In the case of clutter, we can prevent having a mess if we never start what will later be a mess. We must throw the junk mail away as soon as we get it, take one item out of our closet to donate each time we get something new, and go through our email files every day and decide what to discard. We must adopt the attitude that we never put off until tomorrow what we can do today. We have to look for short segments of time to clean out a drawer or go through a pile of papers.

As in Linda's case, she taught her students to go through their desk every day in order to be ready for the next day. At the same time, she was getting them in the habit of throwing away in preparation for the next day. We have to form the habit of prevention.

We all can be a role model for our family members and our friends. We can do this by showing others we have it together by never letting things get out of control in the first place.

Talking Ourselves Through the "I must have it or else!" Crisis

We may spend lots of money on storage closets. We have our counters full of junk. We can never find anything on our desk because we have too much paper. We find our lives bulging at the seams because we love to shop, whether physically in the store or while shopping online. Merchandisers know what they are doing. They run ads on television, they run special sales and there are television shows that stress that you cannot live without an item. Perhaps the store tells customers there are only 50 new computers, so hurry to get one of those. It appears we have been brainwashed or tricked into believing that we must have an item. The point is we need to learn to live without those items and need to exercise control.

We need to recognize how advertising works. We are being pressured to buy more items, so many of which we do not need and never did need. We purchase kitchen gadgets have we bought and have never used. Think about how many times things were purchased on sale and when we got it home, we really did not like it and only bought it because it was a bargain. It is not a bargain if we do not enjoy it in our home, or leave clothes in our closet we do not like.

Consider a young woman who bought a new home, and then discarded everything she owned from her previous home because she wanted everything to be new. Buying can make you feel good, but it is also addictive as the natural chemical dopamine is released into our bodies and makes us goal-oriented (Sinek, 2014).

When you are facing the temptation of a purchase, ask yourself these questions:

• Do I already have something similar? If so, do I need another one?

• How many times a week will I use this appliance?

• Is there a specific event for which I need this new dress?

• Do I have a place to put this item?

• Do I really need to buy this book or can I get it in the library?

• Am I willing to throw an item away that I already have so I can have this new item?

Yes, we do need to exercise control and sometimes that is difficult but if we can ask ourselves these questions before we buy an item, we can make a lifestyle change.

Setting Small Goals

Imagine you have decided to clean your attic. It is a mess and you cannot walk in it to get what you need. You and your spouse decide that your goal is to have the attic cleaned by the end of the summer. You both are proud of yourselves because you have set a goal. What happens when you have set a big goal and then decide you cannot clean for a few weeks because the attic is too hot? Another excuse might be is that you cannot clean it out because you are going on vacation. You have set a goal but you did not break the goal down into small steps. A large goal is commendable but unless you break it down into small steps, you are not likely to meet it because you will engage in avoidance behaviors.

In education, when children are having difficulty completing tasks, we break the tasks down into small steps. When a child succeeds in one of the steps, they feel good, the teacher and parent reinforces him, and the child is encouraged to take the next step. The child becomes confident because he achieved one of the steps.

We have to adopt this educational practice with ourselves. We have to take baby steps to get to the big picture goal. We are not going to see miracles overnight. If the attic is a mess it did not get that way overnight, and it will not be cleaned overnight.

How do we take those baby steps? We have to start with small achievable goals and we have to write those down. For the attic issue this could involve sitting down the night before to write the steps that will be taken.. We make sure that what we write down is something we know we can do. We might write down that we will each spend five minutes cleaning the attic. That is achievable for us. That day, we might even set a timer to know when the five minutes is up. As a result we achieve our baby step goal. We are pleased. That night we set a goal to clean for another five minutes the next day. What may happen is that we will start and spend more than five minutes cleaning. It is important to set small achievable goals that set you up for success.

Getting Assistance from Others and Learning from Them

You may want to ask your spouse or your children to assist you in a cleaning clutter project. It may be more fun to do a project with someone else. Critical to the process also is that you may have to have their assistance because some items you would like to toss may not be items they want to part with.

In the example of the attic project, if the husband and wife both have items that belong to each of them, they have to work together. If a wife decided to do something alone and threw away some of her husband's items, she might find herself with an upset spouse. Before the wife throws anything away that belongs to her husband, she needs to tell him that she is going quickly through his things, which might possibly result in a willingness to help with the cleaning project, especially if it is a very short project. Most people are willing to give five minutes of their time for sorting and pitching.

We know some individuals who have accumulated lots of rough draft papers or thesis papers and have wanted to throw them out so they have held bonfire parties where everyone brings a box of papers or files they want to sort through, and they burn up what they do not want. Soft drinks or a little wine may make purging stuff easier to do. Make throwing things away a social and fun event.

Learn from others as well. When I was in graduate school, I had a friend who was the most organized and clutter free individual I have ever seen. I watched her to figure out what her key to success was. Essentially she planned everything for the next day the evening before. She even set her table for breakfast the next morning the night before. She cleaned up everything the night before she went to bed. I also noticed that at the end of her work day as a school social worker, she spent 10 minutes throwing things away she did not need and filing methodically what she would need. She always knew where everything was because she was so well organized. She did not put off until tomorrow what could be done today.

Once you accept Decluttering as a way of life and take the above steps, you will find yourself with a sense of freedom and accomplishment because you have made decluttering a habit.

Reference:

Sinek, S. (2014). *Leaders eat last.* New York: Penguin Group.

Chapter Two
Why Decluttering is Necessary

Mari was facing many major projects. She was getting ready to teach her literature classes at the high school, she was writing a grant, and she had a newsletter due for her church. Her office space at home looked like a war zone. She had papers and files all over the place. It was now August and the newsletter was due in two days. Every time she looked at the mess, she got upset. She had always identified herself as being very organized and never missed a deadline. What was happening to her? She was overwhelmed and knew she needed to get her work done but each time she went to her office area, she could not face the mess and found herself engaging in avoidance activities. It was easier to bake her husband a cake or go shopping with a friend rather than to get to work on her projects. She found herself making excuses about why she was not going to be able to make the newsletter deadline. She might not be able to finish the grant. Maybe she would wait and go to school a few days before the year began to work on her literature classes. She just had too much to do and to tackle the projects was just too much for her. She could not figure out why she was avoiding her projects. She had always been able to multi-task before, but could not do it now.

Have you ever felt like Mari? Have you felt like you were frozen in time and just could not get your work done but were unsure of the reason for it? You know you capable of being a productive individual but lately you just cannot seem to get anything done. You are spinning your wheels and do not know why.

In the case of Mari, her office space was a mess. Papers were all over. She had always prided herself in being organized and being able to get everything done. She needed to stop right away and declutter. Decluttering was keeping her from being organized and efficient. While she thought she needed all those papers, those same papers were not helping; they were hindering. Rather than going into her work area, she started closing the door. She was not answering emails or tackling her three big projects.

Mari started engaging in escape and avoidance because she just couldn't face the mess. Ask yourself these questions to determine whether you may have problems with clutter:

Do I have food on the counter that causes me to overeat?

1. Do I have my garage full of so many items that causes me to park the car in the driveway or on the street?
2. Do I have so much clutter that I cannot clean around it?
3. Do I have such a mess in my office or home that I do not choose to invite friends or relatives over?
4. Do I lose items and spend so much time looking for them that I am late for appointments?
5. Do I have so much stuff that I avoid looking at the mess and avoid doing anything about it?
6. Do I have so many items in my closet that I have run out of space?
7. Do I have so many files that I have to purchase another file cabinet?
8. Do I have so many items in disarray that my friends, family, or students seem bothered to be in my environment?

If you have answered yes to at least four of the questions, consider the need for changes in your life.

Productivity Prevention

We all know people who have papers all over their work space and clothes stuffed in their closets. They claim they have a method to their madness and know where everything is; even though they have a mess. However when one watches those individuals, they find it takes them longer to find the piece of paper they need. They could have sworn they had two pairs of white capris to wear this summer but they finally give up and keep washing the same pair over and over again; or even worse, they go out and buy another pair, because they cannot find what they need.

Losing items and being disorganized reduces our productivity. We cannot get a job done because we are spending time finding things in our mess or we just give up and do something over because we cannot find it.

We can increase our productivity when we know where everything is and can find an item quickly. We increase productivity when we have everything we need and have it well organized. Organization increases productivity.

Inducing Stress and Anxiety

Did you always consider yourself a neat individual and you wonder what has happened to you now? You have allowed yourself to become a slave to things such as too many papers, collectibles, clothes, and more because you cannot help yourself. When you see something you want, you feel like you need to have it. You are not a hoarder by any means but you have many things. When you become so involved in many activities such as volunteering to be secretary of your Kiwanis chapter, acting as the historian for another organization, or becoming president of the church guild. You have always prided yourself in your volunteer work, but now all of this new work coupled (took out along) with your day job and other responsibilities begins to create stress. If you have children or grandchildren you may have a larger than necessary assortment of toys for them. You look around and wonder how you ever allowed clutter to take control of your life.

Feeling overwhelmed and stressed out can result in serious anxiety. You find yourself worrying about all the mess you have. You find yourself wondering what you can do with all the junk you have accumulated. You do not have the room for the 75 year old history of one organization. When you agreed to be President of an organization, you had no idea you would inherit 22 boxes of materials. You are afraid of throwing anything out because you worry that someone will find out about it and will ask you for a particular document. One answer would be to ask someone from the organization to help you sort it all out.

You have created a situation where you are anxious about all of these responsibilities and you know you need to get your life back in order, but you do not know how. You do not want to disappoint anyone.

Anxiety not only comes from the clutter itself but also comes from your fear that someone will find out that you have thrown something away that you shouldn't have, in their eyes. Your children may find out that you threw one of their precious childhood toys away; even though you asked or begged them to take their toys away when they moved away from home. You asked the members of the organization of which you are president to assist you in going through the files but they just seem to not have the time. You then become afraid to throw anything away and become more anxious.

You have learned that you have become a victim by your willingness to serve your community and organizations. You thought accepting these responsibilities was the right thing to do but now you worry that you took on too much, you worry even more every time you look at all the materials you have.

You have become a victim of your closets. You thought you needed all these clothes; now there is not enough room in the closet and you know you should clean them out but you cannot seem to part with any of your outfits. You are in constant stress and yet you are the one who created it.

To prevent the stress and anxiety that you have created, you have to get your own life in control. If you want to take on responsibilities in organizations, you will need to make clear what material you will keep and what material you will not keep. If you have too many items at work, you will have to look at which of those items are causing anxiety and how can you get rid of them. If you have too many clothes, you will have to decide which you need or do not need.

Yes, these decisions are tough but once you create a plan and stick to it you will have a calm and stress-free existence. Removing the barriers can create a sense of peace.

Harming Your Social Life

You had a friend who wanted to come over to your house. You chose not to invite them in because you did not want them to see the mess you had in your office or in other places in your house. You have not sorted out the papers you have in the great room and you haven't put the wash away. You have newly purchased items still in the bags because you cannot figure out where you are going to put the items. You start looking for excuses to keep people out of your house.

There was a co-worker I knew who was a great cook but she could never entertain because her dining room table was always a mess. She would bring papers home from work, would accumulate newspapers and magazines, and put the bills on the table. She kept doing that until the bottom of the table was not visible. It was her catch-all spot that kept her from entertaining. Friends quit inviting her over for dinner because she never reciprocated.

Picture this scenario. You would really like to go out with your friends but you look at your messes and tell yourself you better stay home and do some cleaning. You do not go out intent on your belief that you are going to clean. What then happens is that you end up finding a multitude of excuses to not clean because you don't even know where to start. You could have been organized and ended up going out with your friends.

A Hindrance to Your Time

Think about how much time you may waste looking for items because you can't find anything because of the clutter. The more items we have the more likely we are to lose them. Spending time hunting items not only causes stress but it wastes the time we could spend doing more productive activities.

When we have too many items, we are spending more time cleaning, more time throwing items away, or more time making trips to the dumpster or the local thrift shop.

When we have a clean and uncluttered home we are not bogged down with papers and other things, we feel a sense of freedom and have the chance to enjoy our lives.

Detrimental to Your Work

When you have too much paper on your desk or too many items cluttering your desk, whether you are a teacher, an office worker, the bank president, you provide an impression that you are disorganized and you may be impressing others negatively. You can easily be perceived as inefficient just because of your clutter.

In whatever position we have we need to provide the appearance that we are efficient, well organized, able to locate items quickly, and we are disciplined. If we have too much stuff, we do not give that impression.

Have you ever gone into someone's office for a meeting and had to move items around just to find a place to sit or you had to move papers around to make a space to write? When that happens, we are losing productive work time.

I once went a couple of hours early to assist a woman as she prepared to give a three hour workshop. I thought when I arrived she would be doing the finishing touches on her workshop and I could help her copy material. I will never forget walking into her office which could best be described as a mess. She was sitting amidst papers and other materials and was totally stressed out. I had the sinking feeling that her workshop might not become a reality, but I knew I had to assist her because there were almost 100 people coming to her workshop. I was able to break the work that needed to be done into a series of steps and directed her on the steps she needed to take and I pitched in and did the other steps. Needless to say, we never had the individual give another workshop. She was under stress and she certainly caused me stress because I do not like doing anything at the last minute and I like all materials well organized.

Impacting Others

Many of our students in today's schools thrive on structure and organization. Some may not have it at home, some crave structure and organization in their lives, and some may have some obsessive compulsive behaviors where they want everything in a certain order or they become upset. If students do not have structure and organization or want everything in a certain order and the classroom is messy, students may not be able to learn. They become so preoccupied with the mess in the environment, they cannot focus on learning.

Students need to know where everything is located so they become familiar with the environment. If things are found in many different places without any sense of order, they may waste time looking for items.

Hazardous to Your Health

Clutter can be hazardous to your health. Ask yourself these four questions that pertain to your health and clutter:

- Do I have so many items around or papers piled up that I cannot dust each item and I risk allergic reactions from the dust?
- Do I have so many items around that I cannot keep them clean and am living it a dirty environment?
- Do I have so much food cluttering my kitchen counters and my refrigerator that I am eating too much or the food is outdated and may be harmful if I eat it?

• Do I have so many items throughout my house that I have to walk around a lot of objects and am creating a hazard where I could fall?

The more we own that clutters our home, office, or any other area, the harder it is to clean. When we live in an environment that is dusty or otherwise dirty we create a health hazard. Have you ever started sneezing when you are cleaning out items? You may have an allergy to household dust. The more stuff we have the more we have to clean and most of us can think of so many other things we would like to do other than clean.

Just as we possess clutter in papers, books, and other stuff, we often have food cluttering our kitchen. Our counters may be full of items. Some of those items have gotten stale. Our refrigerator is stuffed with so much food, we cannot get anything else in the refrigerator and we do not know what we have in there. We forget how long we have had the items in the refrigerator and are faced with the choice—do I eat this or do I throw it away. If we eat it, it may no longer be good and could make us sick. If we throw it out, we have to ask ourselves: "Should we have saved it in the first place?"

There is some work being done that links cluttered counters with weight gain. If we make food too handy by having it sit out within our visual field we are more likely to snack on that food. We all know the saying, "Out of sight, out of mind." If food is not easily within our reach, we are less likely to eat it. We tend to put those snack types of food out on the counter. Those are the foods that can cause us to gain weight. When we buy too much food we are adding to the likelihood that we are going to eat it. As much as we want to have that rocky road ice cream, we need to ask ourselves whether we want to even bring it into the house. If we do not buy it, we cannot eat it.

A recent study from Cornell University and its Food and Brand Lab found that a cluttered kitchen can often cause stressful feels and increased snacking. The combination of stress and a messy environment can lead to more snacking.

(Hayes, 2016, retrieved from: http://news.cornell.edu/stories/2016/02/kitchen-mayhem-can-be-diet-killer-study-says)

Have you ever used the steps or a ladder to put items on? You see a good storage location as the steps while not thinking ahead and it is easy to fall on steps and by putting items that you have to walk over, you are increasing the likelihood that you could fall. If you have your closet stuffed full of items and open the closet door, you may be greeted with an onslaught of items. Have you ever had something on the floor that should have been put away, but you did not do it, and then you tripped over the item? These actions on our part can be hazardous to our health.

Harmful to Your Family

An early study (Evans, Lepore, and Schroeder, 1996) found that a crowded home environment resulted in family members increased withdrawal behaviors. Individuals in the home couldn't cope with the mess and the crowded environment, so they just escaped or avoided because it was easier than facing the mess. Another study (Regoeczi, 2002) showed that when a neighborhood and homes were crowded, children exhibited higher levels of aggression and higher instances of withdrawal behavior. Thornack and colleagues (2013) suggests that clutter may operate in a similar way as cleanliness does as an environmental stressor. These researchers found that home clutter was strongly related to child emotionality and therefore maternal tenseness and, as a result, authoritarian parenting. Such parenting may occur because clutter becomes a stressor on the parent. Clutter and a mess "may serve as a source of negative stimulation that elicits an emotionally dysregulated response in some children." (p. 790). The child acts out because of the clutter and the mother who is already tense becomes more authoritarian.

Expensive

Clutter is expensive because it means we have been purchasing items we do not need. We have magazine subscriptions, newspaper subscriptions, and junk mail. We have our closets full of clothes we bought because we just have to have the new dress, or a better fitting pant. We may also have collections of items. Some of those collector items have cost us a lot. We tell ourselves that we are investing and that the items may be worth more in the future. However things that are still available to use from the past today, such as an entire collection of beanie babies for $15 make us realize they are not huge money makers. Some even have collections complete with the boxes to supposedly make the item worth more money. Whether or not that is true remains to be seen.

Parrish (2010) reported that the concept of accumulating goods is seen as the way to happiness and that the idea has become more prevalent because we believe that we have to compete with our friends and neighbors and the more we own the better. In the "olden days" there was a general store that had needed items. Now we are bombarded with advertisements on the billboards and the internet. We walk in a store and there are many items to choose from. We have more available to buy.

Many of you reading this book have collections and some collection are fine if we are enjoying them and they bring joy into our lives, but if we are not and the items have become dust collectors they were not only expensive, but a nuisance to clean and store.

If we want to save money, we need to ask ourselves whether we really need the item or can we do without it. We need

to also ask ourselves where we are going to store the expensive item.

I can remember needing a new iPad and a sale was going on at a local store. I arrived early to wait in line for the item. While in line, I was talking to a woman who was recently laid off from her job and was having trouble paying her bills, yet she wanted an iPad. I remember wondering to myself why someone who had lost their job and could not pay her bills wanted to purchase an electronic item. Perhaps it is not much different than those who own collections or items, or a closet full of clothes and complain they do not have enough money. Even if we have the money, we need to ask ourselves, "Do we really need this, and can we afford it?" Perhaps our money would better be spent on something else.

We hope you will rethink your clutter and will understand why Decluttering is necessary to lead a more productive, happy, and healthy life.

References:

Evans, G., Lepore, S., and Schroeder, A. (1996). The role of interior design elements in human responses to crowding. *Journal of Personality and Social Psychology, 20,* 41-46.

Hayes, M. (2016). Kitchen mayhem can be diet killer, study says. *Cornell Chronicle, February 3, 2016.*

Retrieved from:

http://news.cornell.edu/stories/2016/02/kitchen-mayhem-can-be-diet-killer-study-says Parrish, K. (2010). Curing the clutter epidemic. *Saturday Evening Post.com, Jul/Aug 2010*, 45-46.

Regoeczi, W. (2002). The impact of density: The importance of nonlinearity and selection on flight and flight responses. *Social Forces, 81,* 505-530.

Thornack, C., Nelson, L., Robinson, C., and Hart, C. (2013). The direct and indirect effects of home clutter on parenting. *Family Relations: Interdisciplinary Journal of Applied Family Studies, 62 (December 2013),* 783-794.

Chapter Three
Throw as You Go

Lilli, twice widowed, began downsizing with the disposal of most things male in her house, although she did create a tool box for herself knowing full well that she might have need of some basics. Her initial activity consisted of disposing of clothing items to places like charities, friends or family. Having done that left her with additional closet and shelf space and without even thinking about it those spaces were refilled and remained so until she retired. Upon retirement she took a closer look at the space in which she had raised her family and knew it was foolish to continue living in such a big house as she rarely had overnight visitors, had cut back considerably on entertaining and began exploring new avenues in which to occupy her time. Her decision to move into an apartment called for serious downsizing but was not without its perks. For the most part she was free of many maintenance chores but before the move began, things had to be sorted and removed. A garage sale was one solution, but there were always things that did not sell but she was able to find outlets that would take most of those off her hands.

That done, her new life began, new circles of activity occurred and within a few years she began dating; hence, the second marriage, the end of apartment living and upsizing into a house even larger than the one she had previously sold. Space simply had a way of getting filled. By the time she was widowed the second time, she had decided on an entirely different lifestyle and moved into a retirement community. She had had experience with downsizing and went about the process with confidence, adopting an altogether new philosophy, Something IN, Something OUT. (Mellon, 2010).

Perhaps you have visited one of the homes designed by Frank Lloyd Wright. He actually designed houses so they would hold a minimum of furniture in an attempt to discourage people from bringing in extra furniture. His houses were built to include built-ins like bookcases, benches, tables and storage chests. In the book *30 Days to a Simpler Life* (Cox and Evatt, 1998), the authors comment that "space is valuable." The things we own necessitate our paying a storage fee, even if that fee is maintaining the space to say nothing about renting a space or buying plastic tubs for storage! Speaking of tubs, they really are smart ways of containing things to be kept, but be sure to they are all a uniform size because they are easier to stack. Create a label and an index of the contents for each one.

Decluttering is not easy to do. It is not something you can do once and be done, although once we have organized and made a place for everything, we need to make a plan to continue. We are not born with an organizing gene. Many times we have found ourselves in "coupon mode" or considered other sales offers such as "buy one, get one free" or "half price offers" and before we know it, the space we have allotted for certain items is crowded. This in turn makes ease of reach or removal difficult. As things are moved or hidden from view we find we have more of the same items. Think about cleaning products and take a critical look at what is actually used. Do you need floor shine products if most of the house or apartment is carpeted or ceramic tile? Perhaps, like Lilli, you are in a complex where lawn care, snow removal, window cleaning, and even general housework, is part of the package. Unneeded items need to go.

The same can be said for many items of personal hygiene. How many bottles of shampoo, bars of soap or body wash are really necessary? If you find you have several, sort them by kind, put the fullest ones to the back and vow to use them entirely until purchasing more. Coupon offers are bound to come along again. Simply call a moratorium on shopping for anything other than food products or medicine for a given period of time. You will be surprised at the effect this behavior will have on the number of purchases you will make.

To review:

- Take stock of what is on hand and use it up.
- Do not fall for coupon or special offers if something is not needed.
- Freebies are not our friends. This includes extra tote bags, water bottles, etc.
- Get rid of any product you no longer use.
- Call a moratorium on shopping except for food and medicine for two months.

Consider closet space. Just exactly how many white blouses or shirts are needed? How often has each one been worn? Someone has said we wear 20% of our clothes 80% of the time. You may not think that is true until you take a close look at what you have really been wearing. An acquaintance read Marie Kondo's book, *The Life-Changing Magic of Tidying Up (*Kondo, 2014*).* She began reading rather casually until something caught her eye and she was challenged by Marie's basic motto that if something hadn't "sparked joy" in her thinking, it needed a new home. That's when she threw open a closet door, took out everything and began sorting. To her surprise she found many duplicate things of the same or similar color, some still bearing the price tag because it had never been worn! Many things no longer fit. They needed a new home for sure! Now that she had reorganized the closet with similar colors together, long and short sleeves in their own special place, etc., she no longer comes home from an afternoon of shopping with something she already has. Another revelation of the closet purge was the bulkiness of many hangers being used. Find your favorite and use only one kind of hanger.

To review:

- Take everything out of the closet.
- Sort everything by type and color.

• Try on anything you are concerned about. If it does not fit, get rid of it, even if you hope to lose ten pounds.

• Get rid of empty hangers and remember use ONLY ONE kind of hanger for everything.

• Give those old clothes to the charitable organization of your choice and think about the joy that someone else will get when they get one of your outfits.

Paper is one of the most challenging bits of clutter for many people. Remember Lilli's determination to make some significant changes? She looked at all the magazines that had accumulated. How many did she actually read? Why was she hanging onto them? Many went into the recycle bin right away. Others contained puzzles or recipes she really wanted to keep so she clipped them out, filed them sensibly and tossed the rest of the magazine. The same was true for all those catalogs crowding the mailbox. A simple phone call got her name off the mailing list within a few weeks.

A **TODAY'S NEWS** article (Miller, 2/10/2016) titled *Savvy Living* offered advice on what to keep and what to toss.

Toss:

• ATM receipts and bank-deposit slips as soon as they have been matched to the bank statement;

•Credit card receipts unless needed for warranty proof or something that may need to be returned.

• Utility bills after the following month's bill has arrived showing your prior payment was received.

• Shred anything that shows personal information. A crosscut shredder is best.

Keep for One Year:

- Paycheck stubs until the W-2 form arrives and is reconciled for accuracy.
- Bank statements once form 1099 is confirmed.
- Brokerage, 401 (k), IRA, and other investment statements once the annual summary arrives. If these show gains or loss, you may keep them longer.
- Health care bills in case you qualify for a medical deduction.

Keep for Seven Years:

- Documents that support your tax returns including W-2s, 1099s and receipts canceled checks to support deductions.

Keep Indefinitely:

- Tax returns with proof of filing and payment should be kept for at least seven years.
- IRS forms filed when making nondeductible contributions to a traditional IRA or Roth conversion.
- Retirement and brokerage account annual statements as long you hold the investments.
- Savings bonds until these are redeemed.
- Loan documents until the loan is paid off.
- Vehicle titles and registration information as long as you own the vehicle.
- Insurance policies as long as they are active.
- Warranties or receipts for big-ticket items as long as you own them.

Keep Forever:

- Personal and family records such as birth certificates,

marriage license, divorce papers, Social Security cards, military records and estate-planning documents. These are best kept in a safe-deposit box or a fireproof safe.

Some documents may be digitized by scanning them to your computer and converting them to PDF files. Be sure to use a backup system such as a USB flash drive or external hard drive like *icloud.com.* If you have found a good journal article and don't want to throw it away, stop and think that the article will probably be available on the web; so if you really need it you can access it. Another option is to email the document you want to save to yourself.

Many email messages need to be deleted on a daily basis. Others may be organized into files. The toss as you go applies. As you get junk or have responded to an item, determine whether the email needs to be kept. So many people write an email that says, "Thanks." Read it, enjoy it, and delete it.

If you have not tossed as you went, stop periodically and set a goal. Today I will delete 200 messages or even 50 messages. It is so much easier to delete as you go rather than waiting until you have thousands of unwanted emails.

If you love to read and belong to book clubs books begin to pile up in your home. In some book clubs members are encouraged to visit local libraries to see if book club kits are available for check-out, which does help to reduce the ever growing pile of books in your home.

Electronic devices are good to use to reduce piles of books in your home, although many still struggle with the urge to purchase more books. Ask yourself if you are really planning to read all of the books, or re-read them if they have already been read. Seriously consider using the library because it involves checking out and returning the books. Now there is an idea for Mellon's *Something IN, Something OUT*!

If you remember to adopt the philosophy that you toss as you go and one in, one out, you will find that your life will be easier and less stressful because you will have tamed the stuff monster. Your new behavior will have a positive impact on your budget, on your time, and on your attitude toward shopping.

References:

Cox, C. and Evatt, C. (1998). *30 days to a simpler life.* New York: Penguin.

Kondo, M. (2014). *The Life-Changing Magic of Tidying Up.* New York: The Crown Publishing Group, Penguin Random House.

Mellon, Andrew J. (2010) *Unstuff Your Life.* New York: Avery.

Miller, J. (2016). Savvy Living. *Today's News, 2/10/2016.*

Chapter Four
Where Do I Start?

Alyson has always been known as a saver. Alyson is a teacher and has worked at schools with limited budgets. She has had to hoard copy paper in her room, has saved margarine tubs for projects, and magazines that have beautiful pictures that someday she might use in an art project. Her house is full of items and when she finds herself with no more room in the inn, she decides to rent a storage unit for her extra clothes and dishes. Her Mother recently died and she was a teacher also. She has inherited all of her teaching materials. Some of those materials are important to her so she brings them into her already crowded classroom. She doesn't seem to have enough storage in her room so she has items pushed and shoved in every corner of the classroom.

When her new principal, who is very neat and tidy, comes into her classroom to conduct her evaluation, he looks around at the disarray of books and papers and is clearly bothered. Previously her evaluations have been excellent, but this time she receives a rating of "Needs Improvement." She is in shock. The principal has told her that her room must be cleaned and organized or during the next evaluation she may receive an unsatisfactory evaluation and will be in jeopardy of losing her position as a 15 year veteran teacher.

Alyson is overwhelmed and wants to organize her room but does not know where to start.

Have you ever felt overwhelmed by a mess you have created? Your closet is overflowing, the attic is a mess, and your garage looks like a war zone. You begin to engage in what is known as avoidance behavior. You rationalize that you do not have the time to clean. Alyson rationalized for years; now she is under extreme pressure to do something about her mess. Her job is on the line.

Alyson, like all of us, is a very busy person. She has

made herself believe that she just does not have the time to clean. She has more important things to do. Now she realizes that cleaning her classroom has to be a priority. What does she do? She has to start somewhere but does not know how to begin.

The key is to get started. Another teacher, Erika, has learned that when she wants her students to complete a math assignment, she cannot tell them to get it all done. If she does that, they put their heads down on their desk because they are overwhelmed. They do not even want to try. Why is that? When children and adults are told to get everything done and there is a lot to do, they are immediately overwhelmed and begin to engage in avoidance behavior. Erika has learned that the more effective technique that she has used with her students is to request that her students start their math assignments. When she uses this language, they begin their work and continue doing their work. She is able to move around the room and reinforce them for working. They keep going because they got off to a good start. Erika needs to utilize this strategy with herself to get her classroom cleaned.

The Advantages of Getting Started

Getting a good start makes a big difference in our attitude. If we get out of bed on the wrong side, we are generally grumpy all day, but if we get out of bed on the right foot, we have a more positive attitude about what we can accomplish that day.

When we actually face a difficult task and begin to tackle it, we gain confidence and keep at it. We got started. We took baby steps and we accomplished something. We can do it and we keep going. Think about the last time you started your day with something going wrong, you tried to be positive but it impacted the rest of your day. Think about the last time you got up early and got two or three tasks completed, you hopefully felt good the rest of the day and found that you accomplished more that day.

Most of us are able to identify that we are making excuses and are engaging in avoidance behaviors. We do not feel good that we are doing this. When Erika looked at the mess she had in her classroom and could not find any place to put her new items, she was bothered. Avoidance does not make us feel better about ourselves; tackling a job, albeit how small, makes us feel better about ourselves. We have gained confidence because we have overcome our challenge and made a decision.

We have made a feel good decision; we are going to start taking control and doing something to overcome the clutter. We have overcome the big hurdle. We started. We can now be successful in our endeavor.

Analyze the Task to Know Where to Start

To know where to start, you have to analyze the task at hand. Having just finished reorganizing an attic, one of the authors looked around, analyzed the mess she had, and then broke the task down into small steps or tasks. She decided she would start with the box that was blocking her mobility in the attic. It was in her way. The cleaning of items in that box meant she could proceed with the other cleaning. This box was the priority and the place to start. Once she had that completed she went through the loose objects that had been placed there when she was not sure where to put them. She worked on that box for ten minutes, made a good dent in it in 10 minutes, and then felt more confident when she proceeded to clean out the rest of the box the next day for 10 minutes.

Most people have a junk drawer or drawers and they have to analyze how to start cleaning out the drawer. Maybe the drawer is full of ink pens, rubber bands, sticky notes, or tape. When we analyze the tasks that are needed with the drawer, the priority is the ink pens because they are taking up so much room. Taking ten minutes, to go through the pens, determining whether they still write or whether they remind us of a trip will then give us more room in the drawer quickly.

Ten minutes got good results for us and made the rest of the job easier because many of the pens were out of the way.

When you task analyze, you always want to look at the first thing that needs to be done that will make the rest of the cleaning process easier. The more you do the more you can get done. One of the things that you also find is that you see immediate results. It was amazing to see how cleaning out that one box made such a big difference.

Learn What Time of the Day You are the Most Productive and Utilize That Time

You really need to know as much about yourself and your work style as you can, reflect on that information, and then use that information to be the most successful in decluttering. An important example is knowing when you work best. You may be an early riser, getting up at 5 a.m. every morning and getting things done before everyone else wakes up. You are the most alert early in the morning and may treasure watching the sun come up. You wake up easily and have the most energy at that time. If this is the case, consider starting your 5-10 minutes of cleaning or your one item on the list at that time. Then you are done and have the rest of the day for the myriad of things you need to do.

You might argue that you do not want to wake others in the household by making too much noise. You are making excuses again. Catch yourself and consider what tasks you can do that won't be too noisy. If the basement or the attic is out of control, others may not hear you working in those locations. If you want to clean items out of a bedroom where someone is sleeping, put those items in a box during the day and then go through the box in a quiet location the next morning.

If you are a night owl like some of us, identify that time when you will do your 5-10 minutes of cleaning or your one item on your list. Night owls find that they can get a great deal done after everyone else in the household is in bed. You may find yourself beginning a task at 11:00 at night. You get started and get your energy burst and keep going. You can then plan what you will do the next night and make that list.

In Alyson's case, she either needs to come in early in the morning or stay after school to get her cleaning started. She isn't going to be able to clean her items out during the day when she is supposed to be teaching.

Are you one of those individuals who contend that you don't like either early mornings or late evenings? You work best in the middle of the day. You still need to identify the time that you are the most productive and utilize that time. You may have a few minutes over your lunch hour or in the morning after you have dropped your children at school. You may like to exercise first and then are revved up and feel more productive. Whatever time works best for you is the best time to start your tasks.

Determine if You Work Best With Lists or With Giving Yourself a Time Frame

As in determining the time of day that works best for you, you also need to determine how you work best. Many people operate with lists. They write down everything they need to do that day. Hopefully on the list is decluttering for just a few minutes a day. It only takes a few minutes at a time to get jobs started. You get a great feeling when you accomplished the task you set out to do; not to mention you can cross one item off the list.

You may also be a person who works best with specific time schedules. Some of us like to set a timer. We take the leap. We determine the job that needs to be done, cleaning out the basement or the attic. It appears to be an overwhelming job. However, if you set the timer for only five or ten minutes that you will begin to make a dent in the mess, it is not overwhelming and is doable. When the timer goes off, you feel a sense of accomplishment. You started the task and set a time limit so you would not get overwhelmed, tired, or sick of looking at the library or the basement.

The advantage of starting the task and only working on it for a short period of time is that you won't get burned out. You haven't spent enough time to get burned out. You will gain a sense of accomplishment because you can see progress in small steps. You are going in the right direction.

Use an Event as a Reason to Start Decluttering

It may help you to have an event coming up in the near future to motivate you to start decluttering. Perhaps you are having company from out of town or you want to get ready for school to start and want your house to be well-organized before that time. You may have decided to have a garage sale and need items ready to sell.

In the case of Alyson she had a professional evaluation and was told that her room had to be organized before a future evaluation.

Have you ever had a cleaning lady? If you did, you may be one of those individuals who runs around the house cleaning up your stuff before the cleaning lady arrives. Knowing that someone is coming to clean or to paint or to repair something in the house can motivate us.

An organization was recently having a fundraiser with a group that pays for collections of second hand clothes and books. For each bag of clothes or books donated, the organization received so much money per pound. Board members and others began cleaning their closets so the nonprofit organization would benefit.

You may not care whether your house is a mess until you have an event coming up. Create an event. Maybe someone has asked to have a meeting at your house, or some kind of clothing party. Commit to the event as it may motivate you to begin decluttering your house.

If there is an event coming up plan ahead of time because with small tasks to complete, it is going to take us awhile to get all of the work done. The stress of putting anything off until the last minute Is not worth it. Start cleaning for the company, or for the party you have agreed to host, or for the meeting at your house. After the meeting is over, you will feel so much better that you managed to have the cleaning completed.

Determine Whether You Need to Have Family or Friend Support or Whether You Prefer to Work Alone

Deciding on whether you want to start your decluttering project with a friend or family member or whether you want to start alone is critical. In many exercise or weight loss programs, the support of others can make a positive difference. You may not exercise alone but if a friend asks you to walk or go to the gym together, you may be more likely to do it. It can be more fun. While it is hard to imagine that cleaning can be any fun, it can make the task go faster if you start on a project together. You can socialize and reminisce about items that you are deciding on keeping or discarding. Picture this bonding activity that took place between a mother and daughter when the mother moved into an assisted living facility.

Margaret had to move into an assisted living facility because of her failing health. She had left a large home behind. With help from family and friends, she was able to donate furniture and clothes and she brought to her new one bedroom home those items that she treasured. She had over six containers worth of jewelry. She just could not bear to go through those boxes.

One day her daughter, Tinley, was visiting and suggested they start going through the jewelry together. Tinley explained that she wanted to hear the story of each piece of jewelry. They agreed to start and work for 20 minutes. Tinley would pull a necklace out of the box and ask her Mother about the jewelry. If there was not a story to accompany it (who gave it to her or where she wore it), or if Margaret could not explain why she wanted it, Tinley suggested they give it away. Margaret agreed and found it easy to part with the jewelry that held no sentimental value to her and that Tinley did not want. They agreed that those pieces of jewelry would be offered to other relatives, and if they did not want them they would be given to a charitable organization. When there was a sentimental story about a piece of jewelry, Margaret would tell the story and Tinley would take a picture of the item and write the story down. Later Tinley made a booklet of the pictures and the story as a gift to Margaret and to their entire family.

Tinley and Margaret began a task that neither was looking forward to, but as it turned out it became an important bonding time between them, and one that Tinley never forgot after Margaret passed away. Margaret had treasured the time with her daughter. What could have been a painful event done alone became cherished moments and created a document that future generations would enjoy reading.

While it may seem hard to believe, initiating a cleaning project with your family can be a time of bonding and doing a worthwhile project together. If the time is with your children, you are teaching them the importance of periodically cleaning things out and simplifying their lives. Children are more likely to help you if they think it is a short project for which they only have to give a few minutes of time. You can all talk together as you clean. As you decide what to keep and what not to keep, you can reminisce about the memories.

If you have a close friend, you may agree to help each other. One day you will work together for a short while with your friend to assist her or him in decluttering. On another day, your friend will help you. You can also consider having an informal cleaning contest with the winner being the one who can fill up one garbage bag a week, or the one who donates the most items to charity each week.

If you are an individual who believes you have to undertake the task of decluttering by yourself, you have flexibility to determine what time works best for you, how you want to approach the beginning of the task, and what items are important to you and what items you can really live without. The key will be to start the project and hold yourself accountable. You may want to graph your progress or take a picture of your progress along the way.

A Checklist to Help You Decide Where to Start by Asking Yourself These Questions:

- Do I need to start in one spot in order to gain access to another spot? Think about the attic example, there was a box that was preventing mobility. That box was the place to start.
- Is there any part of this job that I like to do? Perhaps you love testing pens to see if they still write or perhaps, you love to throw away any rubber bands you have. Those would be the tasks you will want to start because they bring you some pleasure.
- Is there an item that I need to find? Someone has asked you whether you have a large framed picture of Aunt Susie. You think you have it up in the infamous attic but you aren't sure where. While looking for the picture of Aunt Susie do not just root through items until you find it. Instead as you see other items that perhaps you wonder why you are keeping them, throw them away. You may find Aunt Susie's picture which has been hidden by lots of other junk and you also threw away some of that junk.
- Is there a part of the job that is easiest? When Sally was faced with the ultimatum of cleaning and organizing her classroom so she did not get fired, she looked around her room at what might be easiest for her to do? Her perception was that the top of one of her five file cabinets would be the easiest because she thought she had a lot of papers up there that she was no longer using and could toss. It is always a good idea to start with an easy task and we will discuss this more in a later chapter. Why is that? Because we immediately get reinforcement when we see what we have accomplished and that motivates us to keep going.
- Is there a part of what you need to do that is bothering you or someone else the most? Perhaps there is a junk drawer that is

out of hand. Perhaps you have no more room in your closet and would really like to see what you actually have. Your closet is driving you nuts and is interfering with what you are wearing every day because you cannot find your favorite outfits. Consider this and then look for an easy part of this task and get started.

Starting the process of decluttering is a big first step. You are now on your way to eliminating the unnecessary stuff you have accumulated.

Chapter Five
Managing Your Own Behavior To Declutter

Bella has her basement and her attic to clean. Both her basement and her attic take up the whole length of the main level of the house. They are full of boxes, supplies, her children's old furniture, and the list goes on and on. Bella and her husband want to sell the house. The realtor told them that they will need to organize those spaces to make the house more marketable. Bella's husband has major health problems and is unable to help. He has told Bella just to pitch everything. Bella's two children live out of state and have also told her to pitch. Bella faces a monumental task but wants to get the house ready to sell in 30 days. Bella uses the jump start method to help her get started and that is helping.

Bella was a teacher of students with behavior problems so decides to use behavioral principles on herself to get these tasks done. She loves to play bridge but realizes she may have to curtail her games for a while. Then she rethinks that and decides to reinforce herself when she cleans for 30 minutes, then she can go join her friends to play bridge. She also has figured out that she needs to gain momentum for cleaning. She has to rev herself up to clean so she chooses one small box to go through, she does so and then moves on to another easy task—throwing out rusty garden tools. When she finishes that she moves on to another easy task—pitching two outfits she doesn't wear anymore. She is really feeling good about what she has done so she moves on to a harder task, going through a bigger box that has sentimental items that belonged to her parents and grandparents. This box was a bit painful to sort but she is proud of herself that she did it. After doing the hard task she decides to go through a box of broken vacuum cleaner parts. Once she gets this done, she looks around very pleased with what she has accomplished. She is so excited and now feels like she can take the time to go play bridge with her friends. She tells her friends all she has accomplished. They really praise her for having the guts and stamina to clean.

Bella learned effective behavior management principles when she taught. When faced with the difficult task of cleaning out her basement and attic, she decided that she should apply those principles to herself. Just as her students were faced with difficult tasks each day and were successful when she utilized behavioral principles to encourage them, she realized she should utilize these principles on herself.

The Premack Principle—otherwise known as Grandma's Law

Did your Grandma ever say to you? "Eat your peas, then you can have a piece of pie." Grandma was using the Premack Principle. The Premack Principle came from David Premack back in 1959. (Jaspers, Skinner, Williams, and Suecker, 2007). The premise behind the well- researched concept that was found to be effective with children in school from elementary school through college was that a non-preferred activity, like eating your peas, is followed by a preferred activity like eating a piece of pie. (Johns, 2015). Think of the principle as this--first you do something that is not a favorite thing to do followed by getting to do something you really like to do.

In Bella's case, she began to make a dent in her basement (a non-preferred activity) and then she got to play bridge (a preferred activity).

As you utilize this strategy in your life to declutter, look for things that you really like to do and then reward yourself. You may have finished your final exams in college or grad school and then you celebrated by going out to dinner or going shoe shopping. You were using Premack principle to reward yourself. You may have had to go to the dentist and then when you finished getting the root canal, you went to get a milkshake. We all probably utilize this strategy but never realized how effective it has been found to be and how it has been researched.

Some people also call this "The First, Then" Strategy (Johns, 2015) because you first do the non-preferred activity and then you do the preferred activity.

Premack principle is best used as soon as possible after you have completed the non-preferred activity. You don't want to say I will clean the basement for 20 minutes and then next week I will go shoe shopping. The more immediately you reinforce yourself the better. It is also used when you have chosen a preferred activity that is really reinforcing to you. Imagine if you complete your non-preferred activity and your husband suggests that you go to the grocery store and buy your favorite food. However, you are on a diet and do not want to buy your favorite food which is ice cream because it will blow your diet. You have to know yourself and what is reinforcing to you at the time.

Reinforcement

The key to any type of reinforcement is that it be as immediate as possible. We can reinforce ourselves through the Premack principle with a particular activity, the basis of that strategy. You do a non-preferred activity and then you can do a preferred activity as soon as possible after the completion of the non-preferred activity. The technique is not going to work if you wait a week to do your preferred activity. Most of us want instant gratification. If we have done a hard, tedious task, we need a break and it should be a good one.

There are various other kinds of positive reinforcement that we can use to recognize ourselves for working on our decluttered life. Verbal reinforcement is one type. When we have cleaned out one box we can and should pat ourselves on the back and say to ourselves, "Wow, I did a good job on that. Cleaning this one box really has made a difference." While we make think this is silly to praise ourselves, it is not. It is known as positive self-talk. The more positive statements we make about ourselves, the better. We get a good feeling and a sense of accomplishment. We have succeeded. Maybe no one else will notice but we do.

Verbal reinforcement can come from other people as well. Imagine how we are feeling when we have cleaned out that box or two and our husband or one of our kids' comments about how hard we worked or how much better the basement looks. We are on cloud nine. Someone other than us noticed our hard work. Bella's husband could not help her but he was able to come downstairs and say something nice to her. Someone else not only noticed but said something nice to us. It keeps us going.

We do not have to wait for someone else to tell us we have done a good job. We need to tell them what we have done. "Wow, today, I cleaned out three boxes of junk. I worked up in the attic today and actually made a path so I can walk up there." You might say that this would be a form of self-praise and it would be appropriate to do that because in many cases, your accomplishments will result in others agreeing with you and even inviting you to their home to help them learn how to clean.

We can use verbal reinforcement also to get others to help us. As an example, if you want one of your children to help you lift boxes that you want to sort through, you always need to reinforce the child or adult for helping you. Let them know by saying, "I thank you for helping me lift those big boxes." Never take good behavior for granted, always reinforce it.

One of the common mistakes that is made by many is that a kind person tries to help and they do not do it exactly to our standards so we do not thank them, or point out what they did do well or how we appreciated it. If you do not look for what they did that was positive, you are likely to find yourself doing the task alone. The person who tried to help you might reconsider ever assisting again. For example, if your son helps you get the two boxes down and you thank him for doing that, you don't need to follow the thank you with a zinger like:

"Well thanks for helping me get the two boxes down but it would not kill you to stay here and help me sort them out." That is the kiss of death for future help. Make the positive statement and then stop. You may find that if you make the positive statement, your son will stay and help you because he knows he is being appreciated.

Behavior Momentum

Another effective behavior management strategy that has been well researched with school aged children and can be used effectively with adults in the decluttering process is known as behavior momentum. What happens to a snowball when it goes down a hill? It gains speed and gets bigger. It has gained momentum by starting and then picking up speed.

When we clean we need to build momentum. We are taking on a big chore and we want to pick up speed as we go down the hill until we have succeeded by reaching the bottom of the hill. We get more and more done.

The process of behavior momentum is defined as utilizing a series of preferred and easy behaviors to increase the likelihood that we will be able to follow those preferred behaviors with those that are not preferred. (Lee, Belfiore, and Budin, 2008).

How can we apply this principle to cleaning out the basement? We first identify something that is very easy for us to do as we look to tackle the job. This should be a very short task. First let's say that we are going to get a big garbage bag out so we can throw stuff away easily. Good we did it, we got started with an easy task. Then, let's say we look around and see a pile of old magazines. We decide to throw two of them away in that garbage bag we have. We are now going. We tell ourselves that we can do this. We have this project started. We then look around and see two rusty tools that are not antiques. Easy decision to make, throw them in the garbage bag. Look at what we have done, we say to ourselves. We're on a roll. We have taken three steps to gain momentum. Now we decide that we are ready to take on the difficult task of going through the rest of the old magazine pile. We are ready to tackle the project because we started slow and easy, praised ourselves, and now we are confident we can keep going. We used behavior momentum. We started with three easy tasks and then faced the more challenging task.

The important thing to remember with this strategy is to keep going. What you don't want to do is get the garbage bag out and then take a fifteen minute break until you return to the task. If you do that you will have lost momentum. Using the strategy correctly requires you to do the three easy tasks sequentially in a very short period of time and then immediately tackle the more difficult task. Keep the momentum.

Behavior Interpersal

You utilized behavior momentum to get yourself going and you are feeling very proud of all that you have done. You keep going and then you give yourself a short break by doing a task that is easy. Educational researchers say that the strategy known as behavior interspersal can be very effective and can be utilized with behavior momentum. Behavior interspersal is the process of mixing within tasks a task or tasks that are briefer or easier than the others. (Johns, 2015). Some individuals also call this behavior sandwiching because you are mixing difficult tasks with easy tasks.

You can start with behavior momentum and then do the more difficult tasks for a while, gain a sense of accomplishment, and then give yourself a breather by doing an easy task. Pretend you are cleaning out that basement and started with the easy tasks, completed some difficult tasks, praised yourself, and then you return to cleaning something easy. We learned that throwing away the rusty small tools was an easy task so maybe you could go back to throwing them in the garbage. Another option might be for you to go get another garbage bag.

Key to this process is to be sure you know your attention span for tasks. While we all think we have a long attention span, we may find that we really can only attend (particularly to a difficult task) for twenty minutes at the most. In those cases, consider your attention span when you decide when to intersperse an easy task.

It is a good idea to use this strategy with behavior momentum because you have gotten yourself going, you find yourself working away, and then you give yourself a break by doing something easy.

A Checklist

Ask yourself these questions when determining whether you are using evidence based behavior management with yourself:

- Do I reward myself immediately when I have worked hard to declutter?
- Do I know what is reinforcing to me?
- Do I utilize what is reinforcing to me for a job well done?
- Do I engage in positive self- talk telling myself that I am doing a good job and that I can tackle the task?
- Am I proud when I finish a small task and brag about what I have done to others?
- Do I thank and praise others when they help me?
- Do I brag about what I have accomplished?
- Do I analyze the project so I can gain momentum by beginning with three very easy tasks done within a few minutes of each other and praising myself for doing the easy tasks?
- Do I immediately keep going after I have done the three easy tasks and tackle the more difficult task?
- Do I give myself short breaks of easy tasks to complete after I have done a difficult task?

In this chapter you have learned how you can take evidence based behavior interventions that are often utilized with students and apply those principles to your own projects. Behavior interventions work successfully with students and now you have learned how to apply those principles to your current task of eliminating your excess items.

References:

Jasper, K., Skinner, C., Williams, R., and Suecker, L. (2007). Effects of problem order on accuracy, preference, and choice of multiplication assignments. *The Behavior Analyst, 8(3),* 347-359.

Johns, B. (2015). *Fifteen Positive Behavior Strategies to Increase Academic Success.* Thousand Oaks, California: Corwin Press.

Lee, D., Belfiore, P., and Budin, S. (2008). Riding the wave: Creating a momentum of school success. *Teaching Exceptional Children,* January/February, 65-70.

Chapter Six
Banning Excuses

Harper had been in a study group with friends and heard about a book called The Five Love Languages by Gary Chapman. (Chapman, 2010). In the book the author described ways that people gave and received love: Words of Affirmation, Quality Time, Receiving Gifts, Acts of Service and Physical Touch. She knew for herself that she felt most loved when she had had quality time with her family or friends. It came as a great surprise when she was in a relationship with someone whose idea of expressing love was the giving of gifts. Almost overnight her apartment took on an altogether different look because of the gifts she was receiving. And it didn't stop there, because some of the gifts became part of a collection, one she had had no intention of starting! But as so often happens, Harper began adding to the collection, using electronic sales, antique shops, etc. as her sources. When the relationship ended, the collected gifts remained. Now what to do? She was in the process of downsizing and there was no place for these recently acquired possessions.

First of all, she gave serious consideration to those items that she may wish to keep and then, using sticky notes, she labeled all the things that had to go. A call went out to friends and family to come for a visit and "shop" for something they'd really like to have. How amazing to find out just what people had been admiring and wanted for themselves as a true gift from her. How easy was that!

For many of us we realize that the need to hang onto things is the fear that they may need that certain something one day. If we really think about it when was the last time anyone needed numerous baking dishes of the same size? How many sets of pliers are needed in one toolbox? Of course, you have had an occasion when the very thing you needed is the very thing you recently pitched. So, go get another one or call a neighbor and borrow it for one more use. Remember to return it!

Does anyone need multiple sets of bed linens? Towels? Dishes? Cookware? Harper took a long look at the linen closet and decided one bedding change was enough; fewer sets of towels worked very well; and because she was not entertaining as she had before, she did not need place settings of dishes for twelve, maybe not even eight. She called a granddaughter and they made a deal to trade dishes! Now she had far fewer pieces in her kitchen cabinets and the granddaughter was excited to have another special treasure from her grandmother, something she could share proudly with friends. A friend was more than happy to buy the sets of matching stemware that had gathered dust for years. The process continued. Community donation centers welcomed new items to sell.

But then you find yourself saying, "I'm saving this for my children." They may, but chances are they do not, so do what Harper did and ask them. She found out that one of her daughters wanted only the family pictures; not all the photographs, but the only the older and more scarce ones so hard to come by in this digital era. It was easy for her daughter to create a digital record for other family members.

Some friends collected porcelain statues for years. They saved the boxes so the statues would be worth more money. They were eager to give them to their children and were planning to leave them in their will for their kids. They told their kids that these would be worth a lot of money someday. Imagine their surprise when their kids told them they had no desire to inherit the porcelain statues. They did not even like them.

There is a lesson to be learned before saying you are saving something for your children: Ask your children whether they want the objects.

Photographs are another issue, and you need to ask yourself how many framed pictures of mountains, waves, castles, and bridges you really need. It is as though some insidious photo bug has infected our society. Now that pictures can be saved electronically, go through them on a regular basis and see whether they are meaningful to you. If not, discard them. Pictures may be more meaningful to some individuals when there is a person standing by the castle, and to others they prefer to have only nature in the photo. If you think the picture you took of the mountain range is stunning, then consider enlarging and framing it. It makes your home unique. The same goes for family photos. If it is exceptional enlarge it and frame it.

Many of us may have pictures from a deceased aunt or uncle or a parent and we are not sure what to do with those pictures. Here are some ideas for you to consider:

- Sort through the pictures and throw away any duplicates or give the duplicates away to another relative.
- Make a collage with multiple pictures and give the framed collage as a gift, or keep the collage and display it.
- Post the pictures on social media to store there.
- Consider writing a memoir about your family and utilize the pictures as a legacy of your ancestry. Every picture has a story and a story can be told with these wonderful pictures.
- If you are not ambitious enough and do not want to tackle writing a memoir with the pictures, then consider making digital albums of the loose pictures and give them as holiday gifts to relatives.

References:

Chapman, G. (2010). *The five love languages.* Chicago: Northfield Publishing.

Chapter 7
Practical Purging with a Purpose

Liz was so eager to get herself organized that she was one of the first people in the door at a seminar on just that, "Let's Get Organized!" She took copious notes on the presentation and was able to put some of the ideas to immediate use. She created specific zones for things including keeping her recycle box in a handy location. That way things did not accumulate because she delivered her donations and recyclables regularly. She trained herself to put things away now, not later. She used labels on her storage bins as well as creating a list of contents in the bin. She no longer saw an empty space as a space to be used for storage. One thing the seminar presenter had emphasized was that flat surfaces were not for storage. How pleasant it was for Liz to walk into her house, and see areas free of clutter that had once been frustrating.

Another helpful behavior Liz created was establishing homes for things where they were most used. Everything was easily accessible. It seemed so simple once she put that idea into practice. She also invested in a file box complete with folders which she labeled for routine paper work and kept that nearby so that when mail arrived, she could sort items as needed and toss any to be recycled or trashed. It was not long before Liz found herself writing checks to pay bills at a regular time each month even though she knew folks who found online banking to be a handy process. She resolved to look into that as a possibility. She remembered one of the seminar quotes by Benjamin Franklin: "For every minute spent organizing, an hour is earned." This was indeed a reward in itself.

Organizing is probably not something any of us learned in school nor were we born with this particular gene. And it is not once and done. It truly is an ongoing process to be set in place, practiced regularly until it becomes a lifestyle.

Meanwhile, there is always something new to be learned, a new method to be utilized. (Rocks, 2001, Reich, 2013).

Beginning with something as simple as having a regular place to put your purse or your wallet when you come in the door is a good start. This way you are ready to see that everything has its own home. This chapter will focus on ideas on "purging with purpose."

Purging with a purpose will make our life easier. If we purge as we go, we organize ourselves and we prevent clutter. Just as we know that prevention can be the best medicine, purging can be the best way to keep clutter from accumulating

Here are some ways we can purge with a purpose of preventing clutter.

Purging Your Purse or Wallet When You Get Home

Many of us get receipts and immediately put them in our purse or wallet or we get someone's card or we write a note to ourselves and we put it in the purse or wallet. Those items can become a dumping ground for all of our information from the day. If we are not careful, our purse or wallet will not close because of our lack of purging items.

The time to clean it out is when you arrive home. Go through what you have accumulated that day. Put the items that are not necessary for you to carry around for the rest of the week or the month away. If you have receipts, file them in the place they need to be. If you received someone's business card, put it in a business card holder, or take a photo and organize it on your computer. If you wrote a note to yourself, take care of the reminder that was there and then throw the note away or delete it from your phone or computer. Otherwise you will find yourself with a cluttered purse, wallet, phone or computer and you won't be able to find anything that you need in a hurry. Purging is critical to what you need to carry around. Your purse, wallet,or electronic devices should only contain what you absolutely have to have each day. Store rarely used digital items on a hard drive.

If you receive coupons for a free items with a purchase you made, and you do not particularly want the free item then give it away as soon as possible, or send digital coupons via email to a friend. You will make another person happy and you will be happier for having less clutter in your life.

Purging Items in the Kitchen

Do you ever put things in the refrigerator and forget about them? You went out to eat and couldn't eat the whole dinner so return home with a doggy bag. You forget it is there until a week later you look in your refrigerator and discover those leftovers. You wonder whether they are spoiled now and are afraid to eat the leftovers. You have wasted the food because you failed to purge things accumulated in the refrigerator. We all have put items in the refrigerator like peaches or cherries and forgotten they were there. When we check them out they may have mold which results in a waste a lot of money because of failure to purge our refrigerator frequently.

Our cabinets may be full of items that have expired because we pushed them into the back of the cabinet and forgot they were there. The cake mix, the vegetables, the cans of soup may have all expired and we are left to wonder whether we should use the items. As part of your purging the cabinets, check the expiration dates frequently and eliminate the items if you believe they are unsafe. We may also have forgotten we have that sack of chips or cookies in the cabinet and then when we discover them they are stale. If we would have checked the cabinets sooner we would not have to make another trip to the store to purchase more.

The kitchen counter as we have discussed in another chapter accumulates a lot of junk. When we have food on the counter, it is too convenient for us to eat. We are tempted to eat it because it is within our eyesight and we then tend to eat it and gain weight. In a recent 2016 study done by Cornell University, it was found that females in a cluttered and chaotic space consumed approximately about 103 calories more than females in a serene environment. (Olson, 2016).

Purging the Paper Mail

With the increase in technology, we do not get as much information in the mail. However we get enough between advertisements, catalogues, requests for donations, and more. We need to go through our mail daily and purge. The easiest way to do this is to purge the mail by the garbage can. That way we can look at the mail, decide what we want to keep, and then throw the rest of it away. It is easier to do this when you are close to a garbage can unless you have already opted to pay your bills electronically therefore reducing some of your mail. Some of you prefer not to do that. If bills are there, put them in a pile that you know is to pay and pay as soon as your bank account allows. When you receive catalogues and find yourself keeping the catalogue because it has a coupon it, think again. Tear out the coupon and put the coupons in a place where they are handy so when you are ready to go shopping the coupons are ready to go with you or use a preferred card or phone app and get the latest discount.

Remember when you receive those perfume ads in mailings that the scents can sometimes persuade you to purchase something even if it was not a priority item until your received it. Unless you really had planned to purchase perfumes for yourself or for another as a gift, resist the urge to buy based on your sense of smell along with impulse. An expensive bottle of perfume may end up sitting around your home not being used which would be a true waste. If you still receive paper bills put them in a pile that you know is to pay and pay as soon as your bank account allows. When you receive catalogues and find yourself keeping the catalogue because it has a coupon it, think again. Tear out the coupon and put the coupons in a place where they are handy so when you are ready to go shopping the coupons are ready to go with you. Some stores now have cards you simply show to receive get the latest discount, or use your smartphone.

It is critical that you don't allow the mail to pile up. Some people keep piling it on their dining room table and they don't even know what they have. When you pile the mail, you are more likely to forget to pay a bill or respond to an important letter. You may miss a deadline for responding about your attendance at a meeting.

Purging Your Emails

Do not allow yourself to be the victim of consumerism via email. If you do not see what is being advertised it will be easier to resist what you are not missing. There is a cure for that known as purge as you go. Many junk emails are easy to purge. Simply unsubscribe or click the delete button. If you must get a separate email account for notices for sales at your favorite stores. By doing that, you allow your regular email system to be devoted to messages that you want. When you get an email and you respond and you don't need to keep a record about it, delete the email. Each day, go through emails and retain only those you need and then purge the rest.

Purge After Meetings

You may attend a business meeting or a faculty meeting or a service organization meeting and get inundated with paper. Immediately after the meeting decide what is important and what is not and get rid of any excess reports, particularly if you can access those reports electronically. If you need a hard copy to read and some of us do because we don't want to read online, then read, take any notes you need, and destroy.

If you are in charge of a meeting, be very cognizant that in today's world people do not want to be inundated with many pieces of paper. Condense as much as you can before the meeting. Utilize front and back to reduce the number of papers in half and send reports that you can send electronically.

Purge Files Frequently

If we purge information from meetings as we go, we won't have as many files. We can maintain files only for those important papers that we need to keep. However we may have accumulated file cabinets and we keep purchasing more file cabinets. At least once a month when we need to add to our files if necessary we should then be going through the files and seeing whether there is anything else that can be pitched. We may want to keep new files on top of the cabinet and limit the time they can be there one or two weeks. Then at the end of the week, we go through the file cabinet to see whether anything can be pitched to make room for the new material. At times, this is hard, because we think we may just need a file in the future. If it is a memory or a legal document, we will want to keep it. If it is not, we need to ask ourselves whether we have used the file within the last year. If not, pitch it.

Purging Newspapers/Magazines/Journals

We can prevent the need to purge in the first place by deciding which magazines must be purchased compared to ones that we don't need and therefore cancelling the subscription. We may also want to consider subscribing to some magazines electronically on our electronic device. This reduces paper. If you do not want to read magazines electronically and prefer the hard copy, then read the magazine, save any articles you want, and throw the rest away. Many individuals who need references for papers they are writing or research they are doing feel the need to keep copies of the journals where they cited references. An option is to cut out the particular article that was referenced and only save the actual article. Consider also that many of these journals are online so you may be able to access it electronically and therefore do not need to keep the hard copy at all.

There is no need to have stacks of newspapers. Read the daily paper if you read a hard copy and toss it. If there is an article you want to save, cut it out and file it. A good rule of thumb is to throw the article away if you have not used it for a month. You may want to read the newspaper online. If so, that cuts paper quickly but be advised that some do not enjoy reading a newspaper online. It has to be your preference.

If you are still one of those people who searches through the advertisements until finding something you want, be aware of the fact that it is just another way of cluttering up your life with ads and more useless things you do not need. Coupons are a great enticement as well, but if you did not intend to shop for anything this month, you do not need to head to the department or grocery store to buy things you could have done without.

Purging the Junk in Your Drawers

Are your drawers overflowing? Do you have trouble closing your drawers? Whether it is your kitchen drawers, bedroom, drawers, or office drawers, if you cannot close them because they are too full it is time to purge. We need to go through our drawers and pitch or recycle old underwear, socks, papers, and whatever it is that is causing our drawers to overflow. The key question is: "Do we really need all the items in the drawer?" Certainly if we have not used or worn the item in the last year, it is time to get rid of it.

A good time to clean out a drawer is when you are on the phone. You can engage in a conversation while pitching items. Put your phone on speaker and go to work.

Purge Your Storage Areas

We all have storage areas. It may be the attic, the

basement, the closets, the garage, or some other location. We have discussed about the importance of starting on those tasks because they may be overwhelming and we realize that we just cannot purge the mess we have created. Prevention is the key here. Purge a little bit at a time. Pick a corner and purge. A good time to do so is right before your garbage is picked up. Take just a few minutes to fill up a garbage bag and do that every week. Another good time to purge is right before an organization is requesting items for a sale. Maybe you are considering a garage sale. To make any money, you have to purge. Some people don't want to spend the time having a garage sale. If that is your case, consider having a block garage sale. A sale will force you to purge or participating in a fundraiser that needs items for a sale will force you to purge.

Checklist for Daily and Weekly Purging

Daily Purging Needed for the Following:

- Purse or Wallet
- Mail
- Emails
- Newspapers
- Information from meetings

Weekly Purging Needed for the Following:

- Kitchen counters
- Refrigerator
- Storage areas
- Magazines
- Files

References:

Olson, S. (2016). Recalibrate. *Renew, Fall, 2016,* pp. 16-20.
Rocks, C. (2001). *Organizing the good life.* Tempe, Arizona: Facts on Demand Press.
Reich, B. (2013). *Secrets of an organized mom.* New York: Atria Books (Division of Simon and Schuster.

Chapter Eight
Getting It Out of the Box

Beth had fond memories of her in-laws and thought frequently about helping them downsize before their decision to move into a smaller, easier to maintain home. While they were working in one particular closet, she found a small lightweight box, neatly wrapped and labeled "empty box". Could that be true? Cautiously she approached her mother-in-law about it and they smilingly unwrapped the box together. Sure enough, it was an empty box that had been nicely tucked away, supposedly just in case it was needed. Behaviors like that are fairly common among folks who lived through the Great Depression.

Beth didn't think she had any boxes "wrapped and labeled" for future use but she knew she had boxes full of things she had not used in some time as well as empty boxes she might need for holiday gift wrapping. Beth needed a plan, so she googled "declutter" and found a number of helpful hints including ideas about things stored in boxes or bins, shoved into a drawer or pushed to the back of a shelf. She also visited her local library and was delighted to find several books with more suggestions. She knew many things needed to be trashed, others could be donated, many things she would be keeping AND she resolved that anything she kept had to have a home and that might mean relocating them, returning them to that "home" once they had been used.

She called a friend whose house always seemed to be in order, inviting her to spend thirty (30) minutes with her on getting things out of one particular box. She explained her purpose and the friend was delighted, even flattered, to have been asked. Together they made their way through the box of long forgotten items employing some of the ideas she had researched. Not surprising, most things were in good shape, quite usable, but no longer needed by her so these went into the donate category.

Rather than delaying that task she and her friend drove to a local thrift store, donated the items and stopped for coffee. Beth had made the task manageable by attacking only one particular area, enjoyed the company of a friend, and completed one task for that day. This was such an affirmation of her behavior that she was able to continue sorting on a regular basis, realizing that it had to be ongoing rather than a matter of procrastination.

Doing a little every day or so makes organizing a marathon rather than a sprint! It has been said that Dale Carnegie believed that people are rarely successful unless they have fun in what they are doing. Enjoying the company of a friend is only one way to tackle long forgotten boxes.

Sometimes the long ignored box or bin may contain items that simply need to put in a proper place in the home; things like gift or package wrapping supplies, clothing care items (brushes, polish, etc., even the sewing box with scissors, needles, threads, buttons, placed near the laundry area or gathered, stored in a see-through bin, labeled and replaced on a shelf. The creation of a folder with common mailing supplies and placed in the desk drawer is another good organizational tool. How often do we intend to send a note or card to someone but have none on hand? We dash out making purchases again and again. Why not gather a supply of commonly used cards for birthdays, anniversaries, sympathy, get well, general note writing and file them in a box designed for such a purpose. This way you can be organized and ready on the spot, thus saving time and likely money because you are not making numerous trips. You may also want to consider utilizing ecards or apps.

Once you begin going through boxes, you may find you are questioning yourself. What was I going to do with this? How much money did I spend on this? Would I purchase it again? Could someone else use it or need it? We may find ourselves consumed with the idea of loss so we tend to accumulate more in order to feed that need. Sometimes we sense that more is better rather than considering what really makes for a good life.

Have you known people who have things stored in boxes or drawers saving them for "good"? What does that mean? How does that work? Do you have beautiful jewelry that you rarely wear? Organize your jewelry box or drawer and vow to wear those lovely pieces when you and your companion go out for a special occasion. Perhaps you have stemware but are not entertaining as much as you once did. Unpack those things and pour juice, water, wine, or your drink of choice into that beautiful glassware and enjoy it. It is such a treat to cradle stemware in your hand while you refresh yourself, read a good book, listen to music or engage in a chat with friend.

If you purchase comfortable items in different colors do not save them for another day but enjoy wearing the items. Every day is a good day to feel good about yourself and know that you are not leaving things stored in a box or on a shelf. Use the items you have or eliminate them from your life.

One thing that is particularly helpful when it comes to seasonable clothes is an investment in a closet organizer. Depending on just what you enjoy wearing, you may find you do not need a single bar in a closet but one shorter bar hung directly below another one. One area of the closet may even be a series of shelves or drawers. By doubling the space in this way, it may no longer be necessary to store seasonal clothing because you now have closet space for everything. Of course, seasonable clothing needs to be hung where it can be accessed.

What Do We Tend to Put in Boxes and Why?

Books, files, keepsakes such as journals and pictures, and dishes tend to find themselves in boxes. Maybe you have seen a box of books in a co-worker's office that are never utilized. Boxes of books should be distributed to those who will read them.

Recently a retired teacher cleaned out her basement and found a number of books in boxes. She donated the children's books to a school, and the others to a local community library.

If we keep a file box they need to be accessible. If we are keeping the information for historical purposes they need to be preserved in a place that is accessible in addition to being safe and secure. Individuals should check with their local historical society to see if they can utilize the items or can assist in preservation.

A woman was given an old box of a relative's mementos at a time when she was very busy. She put the box in the garage amidst a few other boxes. She was purging information in her garage one day and found a box that contained an 80 year old scrapbook. Newspaper articles were crumbling, writing was fading, unfortunately it was too late to preserve some items but if those items had never been stuck away in a box this may not have happened.

Other individuals have discovered old journals from their parents and don't know what to do with them. Take them out of the box and either copy them or retype them to preserve those memories. Consider making them into a book that can be left for future generations. If they are belong to an organization perhaps the group should consider archiving them or donating them to the local historical museum.

Remove photos of previous generations from boxes and place them in safe materials so that water cannot reach them in case of home accidents. Ask the local museum or genealogical society how to preserve them correctly. Never tape a note or put a sticky note on the front of those photos because of the delicacy of them, and it may cause permanent damage to the photos. Take a picture of the old photos and preserve the memories electronically. This may take a great deal of time depending on how many photos you have, but it would be worth your time to call relatives and set up a schedule to sort through them and decide which items to frame. Another person can provide a different frame of reference when looking at photographs.

A number of individuals find themselves putting dishes they have inherited in boxes. You will not be able to use them this way. If you do not think you are ever going to use the vintage dishes again, but want to have a keepsake of who owned them then keep one or two pieces and showcase those. Consider giving pieces of the rest to relatives. Most relatives do not want an entire set of dishes but they may be pleased to have a cup and saucer as a memory of a loved one.

Getting Out of the Box Party

You may dread going through old boxes of materials. You have let those boxes pile up because you just cannot face going through them. When you are going through the boxes of your mother's and father's old photos, you may want to make a party out of it. Get together with family members and share memories and decide what to do with the items. If you are going through the files of an organization, invite key individuals from the organization to a small party to go through the files and take a walk down memory lane. You can decide who should have what files and what files need to be preserved and which files do not need to be kept. Do not assume all the responsibility for cleaning out the boxes yourself. Make it fun and involve others and the task will seem less daunting.

Holiday Storage

If you have holiday things in storage bins or tubs, make sure to take the time to purge these items annually. It is natural to purchase a few new decorations each year, but this means you need to eliminate some things from your holiday boxes at the same time. If you have found new things you absolutely love, then give some of the older ones to a family member or friend. If they are not interested, then the item need to be donated to someone who will actually use them. It is a travesty to keep items that bring joy in a tote or other place where they are never seen. Label all the boxes as you purge since things will likely be rearranged as you organize. Make it a practice to remove unwanted items the same day you add new ones.

A Checklist to Review:

- Research other sources for organizational ideas.
- Tackle one area at a time and complete that task.
- Engage the assistance of an organized friend.
- Celebrate each completed task.
- Use what you like and get rid of the other.
- Organize first, then invest in storage equipment if needed.
- Organize for holiday storage.

Chapter Nine
The Three Piles

Claire had too many things she had saved from having one child to the next. She had a boy, then a girl, and years later another boy. Life had been a struggle, and money for anything more than food, clothing, and shelter had been out of the question. It was years of taking care of items and then saving them for future use, and so she had not really learned to purge anything.

Eventually she decided to donate the bassinette, the toys, and the educational books. She figured she had done all she could with them as her children had outgrown those things. She had no nieces or nephews to donate them to, and her friends' children had grown up with hers, with the exception of her last son, so she really had no one to donate them to except for the local Goodwill. She set about making three piles; one for discard, one to keep, and one to donate. The old and faded would be discarded, the still good would be donated, and one or two items of baby clothing that still held memories for her would be framed, as well as the small rocking horse she decided to save as a display.

In order to declutter you will have to make three piles before you can move forward. These three piles are essential for you to move towards a decluttered life: One pile is for discarded items, one is for items you will keep, and one is for useful items you will donate. If you find you have a difficult time even getting to this stage where you are creating piles there are a few ways to go about it.

Things that are flawed in any way, such as being cracked, broken, torn, or stained need to be placed in the **discard** pile. They have lived beyond their usefulness. If you find it difficult to eliminate something think of how the item was meant for a purpose, and how it was used for that purpose well beyond its prime. To keep a collection of flawed and unused items is not doing justice to your decluttering. Place these overused items in the trash and move on. If it is a sentimental item like a statue that a relative gave you for a wedding gift and it is broken, take a picture of it so you will still have the memory.

The next pile is the keep pile. The goal is to be highly selective and make the **keep** pile no larger than either of the other two piles. Be very selective in deciding which items to keep. Remember these items will be displayed in a place of honor. If you do not have room for everything you want to keep, remember you will have to narrow it down because again, the idea is to declutter. Sometimes mothers and fathers or grandparents wrongly assume their children or grandchildren will eventually want these items, but often that is not the case. Some people are into antiques and some are not. If you are unsure of this bring it up during conversations to see if they even recall these items. If they have no idea what you are talking about there is no need to save those items for them.

The last pile is the **donation** pile. To fully enjoy the feeling of donating something useful to others, you will need to think of those items you really enjoyed and that are still useful, but that you no longer want or have room for. Remind yourself that there is a purpose for these items, and that their purpose does not lie in being placed in a dresser drawer, or box in your closet or garage. It helps if you come to the realization that living a simple and uncluttered lifestyle will only happen when you clear the way for it to happen. Others who are starting out in life may benefit from a vintage kitchen table, whereas those who are downsizing may appreciate a few items you have in regard to a certain purpose or theme in mind. Allow that enjoyment to happen by giving items away.

Remember that your donation pile can be a wonderful gift to other people. As an example, a school superintendent in central Illinois was a collector of pottery, antique watches, and jewelry. When he and his wife made the decision to move into a small independent living center, he asked his children what they wanted and gave them everything they wanted to keep. However there were many items they did not want. As a result, he had a two ring auction that lasted for an entire day. One of the authors who knew him and had enjoyed working with him went to the auction and bought some beautiful pieces of jewelry from him. She wore those pieces of jewelry and he was thrilled when he heard she was wearing and enjoying the jewelry. When the superintendent recently died and the author went to the funeral, his daughter was talking about his love of jewelry and was delighted to hear that the author was enjoying what she had obtained at the auction. Any time the author wears the jewelry she is reminded of this wonderful man. His donation pile brought joy.

Note that if you have limited room to make these piles, begin with a counter, a closet, or a wall. Not everything has to be moved in one day. You can decide up on a length of time based on your lifestyle. If you work two jobs and have limited time then begin with 15 minutes a day to work on decluttering. You will need to be consistent each day until the counter, closet, or wall is completed.

Also, if you have a drawer, cabinet, garage or anywhere else that needs to be cleaned out, but do not seem to have the energy to begin tackling the mountain of work before you, then break it into workable chunks.

Music moves many to exercise or work to a beat. Whether it is Mozart or rock and roll use it to your advantage. It does not matter how much time you can allot to a task, so if 15 minutes is all you have daily that is better than nothing. Move along to a slow but steady pace and pretty soon you will have that drawer done, then the closet, and the success will spur you on to cleaning more.

Chapter Ten
Making Some Tough Decisions

Erin and her husband Rob had inherited many items after they had helped her parents sell her grandparents' home and move to assisted living. It was mainly due to her grandfather's numerous ailments combined with her grandmother's Alzheimer's.

Erin's parents had already downsized to a smaller place, and they were willing to take a few small items, such as a vintage clock, a few of her favorite necklaces, and her great-grandmother's dishes. The rest was going to be donated to Goodwill after Erin and Rob had taken anything they wanted. As Erin looked through the house Rob reminded her they had a small house as well.

Erin chose a painting she had fondly remembered from her childhood that was always on the wall at grandma's house, as well as a small flowered vase she recalled putting violets in from the backyard there. She could have chosen more, but decided it would be better to give the remaining useful items to someone else who could really use them.

Choosing which items to keep can be a challenge. While you want to keep the important things that bring good memories, it is not easy to decide how many and what.

You can begin by deciding where those items will be displayed. If you have no place for them to be displayed, perhaps another person might have a better use for them. Also, if you are going to keep small items such as a vase make sure it is on display where anyone in the home could see it and admire it instead of placing it in a box where no one can enjoy it.

Think of donations of your most prized items that you have no room for as bringing joy to another person. Perhaps when they own the piece you are letting go, such as vintage tablecloths or paintings you have no place to display, that it will make them happy. That can only be done if you allow it to be donated in the first place.

If you have lots of vintage items you may be able to sell them, but if you do the research it may show that similar items are not selling online. Just because something may be worth a certain price it may take you months or years to find someone who will pay your price. In that case it would be better to give them away to someone who could make use of them rather than letting numerous items clutter up your home for another few months while you attempt to sell them.

Many charities will give receipts for a donation. If you itemize speak to your tax professional and find out what documentation you need to prove you have donated, and also find out how to determine the value of the items to make sure you are taking the correct steps so your tax-free donation will be valid.

Chapter Eleven
Sentimentality

Meghan was close to her parents, and although their passing had been years ago, she could not bear to part with the items that held so many memories for her from her childhood home; dishes, a large box of photos, some of her toys they had kept, favorite clothing her mother had worn, and sporting items her father had used.

Although Meghan knew she had not even looked at these items since her parents had passed years ago. They were still packed in the garage in boxes she had used when she and her husband had moved the items home because she could not bear to part with them. There they had been for 10 years; an unmoving representation of Meghan's emotions.

There were many times when she had considered going to the boxes and sorting through them, but the thought was painful, so she decided it was more of an event she should put off for a rainy day. The rainy day for cleaning the garage had not come in over 10 years.

Objects often hold meaning because they evoke emotion, and most likely the original owner was a family member, a good friend, or a colleague.

Emotions evoked from inanimate objects such as a high school jacket, photo collage, or inherited piece of artwork, often hold strong memories for years. These memories eventually fade over the years, and at some point we no longer find the object as meaningful.

One would think this would eventually lead to our natural purging of these items from our life, and no need to linger over the decision about what to do with it. People find themselves at the crossroad of wanting to keep something of sentimental value, while having the room for all of it poses a problem.

When we have too much of something whether it be

quilts, photos, clothes, knick-knacks, and so on, we have a tendency to rationalize to ourselves why we need to keep it. We may believe that it would be disrespectful or insulting to an individual who gave us the item. Perhaps our children will use it someday, or perhaps we will wear it, or maybe it just needs to be displayed to show respect.

Sentimentalism in the Workplace

Abby was a great teacher many children and parents had loved. She had lots of wonderful and useful items she had purchased over the years for her classroom, and now that she was retiring she wanted to share them. Abby gave most items away to a few colleagues, and a few to a relative who was a teacher. She felt that when she left someone else would benefit from her years of working on items to supplement the curriculum.

Sentimentalism may also exist in the workplace. We may have taken a new job and our predecessor had been in the position for years. We feel like we are the new kid on the block and we don't have a right to throw anything away; yet we want to make room for our own materials. Others in the workplace tell us we can't throw the item away because it is important to the history of the organization. While history is important, we need to be cognizant that everything cannot be kept.

As a new employee, you are walking a tightrope. You want to come in with new ideas while at the same time respecting what has been done in the past. It is easy to set yourself up for failure unless you proceed with caution.

The following are two true stories. An administrator took over a job that someone who had died suddenly had. The previous individual was dearly loved by her colleagues. The new individual came in and proceeded to throw almost everything away that the individual had; some of the material that was pitched was historical and many items were sentimental. The new administrator got off on the wrong foot by taking such action unilaterally and other staff set out to undermine everything she did. After one year, she left because staff never accepted her because she did not respect the fact that the items this individual had meant something to colleagues. What should she have done? She should have recognized that many of this individual's items were sentimental and could have asked other individuals what they would like to have. She should have involved them in the decision making process. She was seen as being disrespectful of the deceased individual's work. She did not need to keep it herself; she could have shared it with others.

In another instance, a new teacher in a small community came in to take the place of a retired teacher who had worked within the school for over 30 years. The retiring teacher had saved, organized, and left several items for the new teacher. The retired teacher thought she was doing the new teacher a favor by leaving her with some of her favorite teaching tools. They were sentimental to the retired teacher and to the other teachers who held the retired teacher in high regard.

The new teacher did not see it this way and threw most of the items away. The other teachers in the building were upset. They thought this was very unkind and disrespectful of the new teacher, and that she had not respected the sentimentality of the previous teacher's materials.

Perhaps the new teacher could have slowly replaced the retired teacher's materials, or have used a few of the items and reported to the other teachers how she had used them. She could have communicated to the retired teacher and thanked her for the materials or told her how she planned to use them. If the materials were not helpful she could have discarded them slowly and might have told the other teachers that some of the materials were not at a level that was appropriate for her new group so the items were available for them to borrow or keep in their classrooms.

Sentimentalism in our Home

If you have saved items in your home that are now in boxes, or stored in your dresser, or in the back of your closet, pay attention: Remove them immediately! Sort through everything and decide which items evoke the most memories for you. Of course all of them have some memories, but we have to choose and eliminate clutter so pick only the best ones to keep. The others will be sent to others to enjoy.

If you have a hard time deciding which ones to send to Goodwill or any other charities because you have concerns about their usefulness, then ask friends if they can use those items, or put up notices on a local website where people search for local items. Sometimes local networks and bulletin boards are places to find out what the needs of the community are. It is better that someone who really needs an item gets the item, such as a set of glasses, rather than letting them get broken in the shuffle to sort things at the local donation drop-off.

Use items that you cannot bear to give away, or create a place of honor for them. For example, if you have a set of dishes that you love, and cannot part with, and that your children do not want to inherit later on for whatever reason, use them now! Grandma would be happy that they are being used! Replacing your present chipped dishes works out for the best. No sense in keeping chipped dishes so change them out now and begin using the vintage dishes. You will be reminded of grandma as you place them on the table every day. Mixing and matching dishes is more acceptable today. Others may notice too as that little smile comes across your face when you think of grandma and the many meals you had together with her.

Chapter Twelve
Displays of Sentimentality

Robert was always close to his grandparents as they had raised him on the farm after his parents had passed at a young age. His grandmother had died a few years ago, and his grandfather had recently passed. As Robert sorted through the items in the old farmhouse he was reminded of the many memories he had on the farm. He wanted to keep many of these items, but since he lived hundreds of miles away in the city, it did not appear logical. Robert decided he would keep and display some of the most treasured items in his city apartment, and that he would donate or sell useful items to local farmers and their wives. All else would go to the Salvation Army.

One needs to be loyal to the memory of a person by removing the items with memories from storage and displaying them in a place of honor. Find a place of honor to display the few items you have kept that you want to remain as treasures. For example, one dish from the set of dishes could be placed on a plate hanger and hung in the kitchen. Medals or awards could be cleaned and polished and displayed in a case. Find someone who knows about these things. Naturally the internet is available, but perhaps a local veteran may be the best person to ask to find out how to display the medals exactly as they would be on a uniform.

In a framing shop, a woman was honoring the crocheted doilies that her grandmother had made as she planned to frame several of the small ones. She then could proudly display the crochet work, rather than having it left in a box where no one could enjoy them.

Find a perfect place in your home to display the item. This could be a wall, a shelf, a table, or a display case. The goal is to honor the memory of a person, and to do it as a clear representation of what your purpose is in displaying it.

If you find you have too many things, such as too many large furniture items resulting in less wall space, then it is time to thin out the furniture. Too much cluttered furniture can be a hazard to your health. There should not be a narrow trail one has to follow upon entering any room in your home. Give away excess furniture to a person who truly needs what you have. This could be anyone from a local college student to a local shelter. Ask around and find someone who can benefit.

Ideas on how to display and honor items:

- Frame old photos, or make copies and create a digital scrapbook for relatives.
- Make a quilt out of old shirts, especially those with patterns or words that evoked memories from the workplace or a vacation.
- Use up the colorful strips of fabric from those grandma kept by tying short strips to light strands.
- Make a collage of old pictures, or frame them in various frames on a large wall in your home.
- If you are fortunate to have old letters that your parents or grandparents wrote, bind those in a book or make a digital scrapbook for yourself and others.
- Find a place of honor in your home for items such as U.S. military flags, historical photos, or scrapbooks.
- Use grandma's old dishes if you are fond of them, as it will bring a smile to your face when you are reminded of her on a daily basis.
- Donate vintage hats or clothing to the local museum or acting troupe. They would be appreciative and it would put those things where they are actually used.

- Give things like pots and pans you have no need for to a couple on a budget, or an elderly couple who are on a fixed income.
- Donate t-shirts and blankets to a homeless shelter.

Use your own creativity to decide how you can display items; get ideas from your friends; go to a framing shop or a hobby store; check out social media. You will find yourself getting lots of ideas on how to display your sentimental items.

Chapter 13
When the Unexpected Happens Create a Grab and Go In the Event of Fire, Flood, or Illness

Margot had retired as a teacher and remained very healthy. She exercised, ate well, and maintained a good weight. She never thought about getting sick because she took care of herself. Margot had no children and her husband and her one younger sister were her only relatives. Her husband became very ill with a rare disease and required a great deal of medical attention. Margot had always thought that her husband would be the one to care for her, and he knew what her medical wishes were.

Margot's sister asked Margot to write down what her medical and death wishes were in the event that something happened to her and her husband. This was very uncomfortable for Margot but she realized that she had better do so; otherwise her sister would be left to guess what she wanted done. Margot compiled her wishes in an official document, kept a copy for herself and her husband, and gave a copy to her sister since she gave authority to her sister in the event that she and her husband were both incapacitated.

None of us want to entertain possibilities of bad things happening to us. We want to believe that our lives will continue with no emergencies or illnesses. Yet we all need to face reality that we could be in an automobile accident, a fire, a flood, or another disaster. We could become incapacitated and no one would know what needed to be done on our behalf.

Planning is critical and we need to have a grab and go plan because we do not want someone else needing to search through all our important papers, many of which might be spread in various parts of our home and our office. We may not know where all of these important papers are so how can we expect someone else to find them.

It is critical to have our important papers in one place, perhaps in a lock box, or at a safety deposit box at a bank, and have at least two individuals charged with our future care have a key to that lock box. Remember that if you do not have a fireproof lock box it may not survive if there is a fire before you arrive home. Also, a small lock box should be attached to the home itself in some way, or hidden, in order that someone not be able to have easy access or be able to steal it easily. Consider these possible scenarios carefully depending upon what you have to store.

If you are not interested in owning a lock box, consider having a bag similar to what some have termed a *Grab and Go Bag*. It is placed in a secure spot in your home along with an extra set of keys, including a key to your lock box if you have one, your will, your passport, the locations of your bank accounts with numbers, your electronic passwords, your birth certificate, insurance policies, and marriage license. Anything else you believe is critical, such as medical information, and find a perfect spot for the bag so it can be easily grabbed by you or a designated relative.

Your *Grab and Go Bag* should contain the following: (Note this is not an all-inclusive list, but rather a list that might make you stop and think about what else you need to include.)

- Passport
- Driver's license
- Birth certificate
- Bank account information
- Insurance policies
- Last will and testament
- Designated papers for power of attorney and designed health care plan.

- Car title(s)
- Passwords
- Keys

While you will not put your credit cards in the bag, you can and should make copies of them and of your driver's license. You should also make a copy of your passport in the event that it is lost.

In the event of an automobile accident you should always have your car registration in your vehicle with a copy of it elsewhere. You should also know exactly where your car title is. Many people keep this in the lock box or their *Grab and Go Bag.*

This bag should be easily accessible to you and your power of attorney so that in the event of illness, the individual knows exactly where the information is. In the event of a flood or a fire, you can grab that information along with your wallet or your purse and get out of the house.

For your important information, you will also want to back up this information electronically on a secure jump drive or secure site. You may want to email yourself the compilation of the copies that you have scanned. Some even like to keep a copy of items in their lock box, or *Grab and Go Bag*, in another location, such as a safety deposit box at a local bank.

Chapter 14
Using Technology to Declutter

Bree operated a small business and utilized technology to write reports and to check and respond to her emails. She also utilized technology to do her budgets. She was still overwhelmed with paper. She kept all of the background information that she collected for her reports in file folders. She kept her receipts. Since she had several accounts for a variety of reasons, she had different passwords but when she needed those passwords she couldn't seem to find them. She loved to read various magazines and journals but never seemed to have the time, so those journals just kept accumulating in her house and her office. The clutter continued to mount but did not know how to curb it.

Bree used technology for her work but she needed to figure out other ways she could use it to her advantage.

Passwords

We are all bombarded with passwords for a variety of email providers and shopping sites. Most of us start out with the best intentions of having the same email for all of the sites but we quickly have learned that different sites require specific symbols or numbers or a mixture of capital letters and lower-case letters. Other sites require changes in passwords on a periodic basis. Many of us write our passwords down in a book and then we have so many passwords that are added or changes, the book gets difficult to monitor. There are secure software apps that are free that will store your passwords. They will keep all your passwords stored for you. You will be required to create one password to use the sites and you will have to update as you change passwords. Another option for you is to make an excel spreadsheet where you keep all of your passwords. Your password access should be available in your grab and go.

Magazines/ Journals

Most of us have at one point or another been overwhelmed by the journals and magazines that we have wanted to read and then left them in piles, hoping that we will have time to read them one of these days. Now, many of those journals and magazines are available electronically and you can subscribe to them this way. This cuts the paper and the piles down significantly. Some magazines automatically renew when we really don't want them anymore. We need to notify those we want to stop and seriously consider whether we really need any of them. With electronic access to so much information, we can find many articles about topics by just googling the topic.

Controlling Advertisements and Catalogues

We buy an item from a company and immediately we are inundated with multiple advertisement flyers and catalogues. How do we stop the hard copy mail? We are getting four to five advertisements per day. If you want to keep some of those, do so. Some of them might include coupons that you really want and others do not. In that case you can unsubscribe using specific software.

Another idea is to create a separate email account just for the purpose of receiving those advertisements. That way the advertisements don't clutter your general email account yet you have another account that you can check periodically for special offers that you may not want to miss.

Paying bills

Some people like to have their bills electronically withdrawn from their bank accounts. This assures that your bills will be paid on time. It also requires that you monitor your accounts to make sure you have enough money to cover your bills. It also requires the careful monitoring that the billing company is withdrawing money out of the right account. Recently one of the authors was confused because she was not receiving a specific service. When she called, she was told that they had stopped her service because she had insufficient funds. Very confused because she knew she had more than enough to cover the bill, she called the bank who reinforced that she did indeed have enough money to cover the cost. She then called the billing company back and they checked the account in which the money had been withdrawn. It turned out that they had reversed the routing number with the bank account number.

Some individuals also prefer to do all their banking online which can also make life easier. You just want to make sure that when you are accessing your information, you are using a secure server because when you utilize free internet when you are traveling, others may have access to your information.

Electronic Record Keeping

Whether you do your banking online or not, you can keep a spreadsheet of information about your accounts. This helps you to not need to keep the monthly bank statements.

You may want to keep a spreadsheet about the location of your insurance policies, your email passwords, birthdays you want to remember, your address book, and other needed information.

Electronic Backups

Some of you may trust that if you backup files on your jump or flash drive, you are saved. However be alert that if those drives are removed from the computer incorrectly or they get old or are too full, those drives go bad and you will lose everything. Do not rely solely on the drives as they can go bad.

While it is fine to back material up on those drives,

have a backup and the safest one is to periodically send the file to yourself as an email. That way you always have it as an attachment provided you do not use up all your memory with your email server.

An increasing number of individuals are utilizing document sharing software which can be shared with others or they are saving things to the cloud. These are additional options so determine what works best for you and utilize that system.

A review of some great ways to utilize technology to declutter:

- Devise a way to keep all of your electronic passwords in one place.
- Consider getting many of your magazines or journals online to reduce the paper clutter.
- Consider auto-pay or banking online as a way to reduce clutter, time, and stress.
- Use a separate email for advertisements or coupons.
- Use spreadsheets or special apps to keep track of your important personal information.
- Send yourself attachments with your important papers and documents.

Conclusion

While reading this book you may have discovered ideas that you had never thought about before to reduce your clutter. Some ideas you may have thought would not work for you while others caused you to have an "Aha" moment. Choose what will work for you and begin the process. You will gain a tremendous feeling of freedom and accomplishment as you eliminate items you really do not need. Streamline and begin to simplify your life!

About the Authors

All three authors have been educators for many years and have served in a number of leadership positions in educational organizations. All three women began working together through Lambda State of Delta Kappa Gamma, an honorary women educators' society, and were encouraged by their fellow sisters in Lambda State to write this book.

Dr. Kammie Richter has a doctorate of Curriculum and Instruction from the University of Illinois at Urbana-Champaign. She has taught in the public schools and has been a cooperating teacher for numerous observers and student teachers. She was named 2011 Illinois Ag in the Classroom Teacher of the Year. She is an active member in the Lambda State chapter of Delta Kappa Gamma International, Key Women Educators, and is a frequent presenter at conventions and conferences. She is an active volunteer in her church and community.

Marilyn C. Myers grew up in Hannibal, MO and obtained a Bachelor of Science in Education from Quincy College (now Quincy University) in 1971. She obtained a Master of Arts degree from Northeast Missouri State University (now Truman University) in 1978 and was certified as a Reading Recovery Teacher Leader by the University of Illinois in 1991.

She has been an active member of her community in many capacities, participated in mission work in Belize, the Dominican Republic and Ecuador and serves at the state and local levels of the Delta Kappa Gamma Society International.

She has been a frequent presenter at conventions and conferences. She is the recipient of the lifetime achievement award of Lambda State of Delta Kappa Gamma.

Beverley Holden Johns has 40 years of experience working with students with learning disabilities (LD), and/or behavioral disorders (EBD) within the public schools. She is now a Professional Fellow for MacMurray College (where she teaches courses on Special Education Law, on EBD, Adaptations, and on Diverse Learners). She also teaches a class on Autism at Illinois College. Johns chaired the 10th Biennial Conference of the International Association of Special Education (IASE) held June 10-14, 2007, in Hong Kong, served as President from 2006 until January 1, 2010, and presided over the 11th Biennial Conference in Alicante, Spain in 2009. She presented the Inaugural Marden Lecture at The University of Hong Kong in January, 2006. Johns is the lead author of 16 books (and co-author of 4 others).

She is co-author with Janet Lerner of the seminal college LD textbook, the 13th edition of Learning Disabilities and Related Disabilities. Johns is the 2000 recipient of the CEC Outstanding Leadership Award from the International Council for Exceptional Children (CEC), Past International President of the Council for Children with Behavioral Disorders (CCBD), Past President of the CEC Pioneers, Past Secretary and Governmental Relations Chair for the Division for Learning Disabilities (DLD), and the 2007 Recipient of the Romaine P. Mackie Leadership Service Award.